casino design

casino design

Resorts, Hotels, and
Themed Entertainment Spaces

Justin Henderson

GLOUCESTER MASSACHUSETTS

ROCKPORT
PUBLISHERS

First published in the United States of America by:

Quarry Books, an imprint of

Rockport Publishers, Inc.

33 Commercial Street

Gloucester, Massachusetts 01930-5089

Telephone: (978) 282-9590

Fax: (978) 283-2742

Distributed to the book trade and art trade in the United States by:

North Light, an imprint of

F & W Publications

1507 Dana Avenue

Cincinnati, Ohio 45207

Telephone: (800) 289-0963

Other Distribution by:

Rockport Publishers, Inc.

Gloucester, Massachusetts 01930-5089

ISBN 1-56496-577-5

10 9 8 7 6 5 4 3 2 1

Design: Fahrenheit

Cover photo and photo on page 6: Star City Casino
    and Resort Complex, by Patrick Bingham-Hall

Section opener photos:

    Desert Inn Resort and Casino (pages 12–13) by Robert Miller

    Harrah's Shreve Star (pages 60–61) by Ian Vaughan

    Mohegan Sun Casino (pages 86–87) by Paul Warchol

    Hyatt Regency Aruba (pages 102–103) by Jaime Ardiles-Arce

    Sun City Hotel and Casino (pages 128–129) by Strobe Photography

Printed in China

CONTENTS

INTRODUCTION: THAT'S ENTERTAINMENT!

By Justin Henderson

Today, when people think of casinos, they think first of Las Vegas, and rightly so. Founded by characters of questionable repute and renowned as the American mecca of gambling and other vices, today boomtown Las Vegas represents the acme of gaming, not only in America but internationally. In Vegas, previously considered evil "gambling" lost a few letters and became respectable "gaming"; the lurid neon sleaze of the Strip and its sin-filled casinos reinvented itself as the world center of entertainment architecture; and all the desperate souls in search of an easy buck or a winning roll of the dice at 4 a.m. were replaced with families, millions of them, strolling the Strip from mega-resort to mega-resort on a sunny afternoon. Within a few hot Vegas blocks, these vacationers visit New York City, ancient Egypt, nineteenth-century France, Hollywood, Paris, Venice, medieval England, Rio de Janeiro, the South Seas, and myriad other times and places. They hang out with cowboys, kings, pharaohs, and pirates; watch volcanoes erupt; and ride roller coasters through the streets of Manhattan.

The design of Las Vegas casinos always depended on fantasy. In the old days, the fantasies primarily came from the imagery and iconography of the desert and the oasis, with some regionally inspired American West motifs thrown in. Flamingo, Tropicana, Desert Inn, Aladdin; you can sense it in the names.

In the last ten years, though, casino visionaries like Steve Wynn upped the ante by changing the rules and the scale. Back in 1989, fifteen years after the last new casino had opened and years before the Vegas skyline debut of New York City (New York-New York), Egypt (Luxor), King Arthur's England (Excalibur), and the "movie set" that is the world's largest hotel (MGM Grand), Wynn's Mirage Resort appeared and forever changed the way the game is played in Las Vegas. When the 3,044-room Mirage opened, followed by the 2,891-room Treasure Island four years later, these two side-by-side hotels represented the first in the wave of mega-scaled destination resort/casinos, with thousands of rooms, expansive public spaces, and most significant of all, a consistent fantasy theme. The formula proved enormously popular, and in the decade since, a plethora of themed casinos transformed the Las Vegas Strip into a fantasy extravaganza, a family-oriented destination that paradoxically derives much of its revenue from a non-familial activity, gambling. For better or worse, Wynn's vision of Las Vegas as the world capital of make-believe architecture proved to be prescient, and following up on those early successes, he is currently masterminding the next wave of even larger, more grandiose themed casino resorts.

Examining these two projects is to get a look at things to come. Not that the Mirage or Treasure Island are dated: they remain among the most consistently popular of Vegas resorts. Condemn this populist fantasy approach to hotel design at your own risk; the world loves it, and seemingly never tires of it. Las Vegas today is the most popular tourist destination in the United States.

After the Mirage came an explosion of more mega-scaled fantasy resorts, their themes drawn from diverse cultures, eras,

[left] Mohegan Sun brings the fantasy of Native American mythology to life in a comfortable theme-resort setting.

and countries, served up to happy consumers as cartoon buildings, replicas of realities those consumers never experienced but instead have seen in movies, on television, in picture books. The details sometimes were a little different from the real thing, but the fantasy worked. Several places such as New York-New York and Luxor feature prominently in this book. They draw crowds. They entertain. They make tons of money. And on the horizon, rising ever higher and growing ever fatter—and easily outscaling the three- or four-thousand room properties of the 1990s showcased in this book—loom the city-themed resorts like Paris and the Venetian, due to open in time for the new millennium. In Las Vegas, it appears that anything goes—as long as the faithful keep coming back for more.

The gaming explosion in the United States has taken the rest of the country by storm as well, and it is the original Americans—Native Americans—who have profited in many cases from this new national obsession. Though few of the Native American casinos demonstrate the imaginative design of the Mohegan Sun in Connecticut [page 90], increasing competition among the dozens of reservation casinos has begun to push the tribes into making more interesting buildings. They've turned to experienced casino planners to aid in design, and they're mixing up tribal motifs with tried-and-true casino tricks in fine style. A few more samples—Harrah's Skagit Valley and Ak-Chin—can be found in this book.

A similar competitive challenge now stirs the action in the realm of riverboat gaming as well, evident in the gaming boats and onshore pavilions shown in this volume. An essay by Paul Keller—a gaming boat and riverside pavilion planner for a major development company—illuminates the history and challenges to be found in this booming segment of the industry, with its Midwestern version of international glamour appealing to older players and other segments of the population.

Overseas, in Europe and more distant destinations, planners continue to mix the quieter, traditional approach to gaming with what they deem acceptable from the glitzy, frenetic Las Vegas. And in the Caribbean, the Las Vegas approach has begun to influence casino and resort planning to a small extent, but with one large exception: the Caribbean properties included herein treat the casino as an amenity rather than the heart and soul of the operation. Given their wonderfully appealing settings and relatively small scale, this surely is an appropriate design approach for the island resorts.

A hybrid art, casino design combines architecture and interior design with a large dose of glamorous theatrics, a serious need for security, and a highly manipulative approach to space planning. But above all, contemporary casino design must amaze and amuse. This is the architecture of entertainment and fantasy. It may not be profound, it may often be two-dimensional or less-than-faithful to the places it replicates—but in the end it's meant to be fun, and if it succeeds at that, the other stuff doesn't matter. Bring on the crowds, and keep the volcanoes erupting and the dice rolling.

LAS VEGAS *and* LAKE TAHOE, NEVADA

The Mirage and Treasure Island Resorts

Architecture and interior design by Mirage Resorts
Photography copyright Mirage Resorts

Developer Steve Wynn started the fantasy-resort boom with the Mirage, which opened in 1989. Architecturally, it is fairly straightforward, a functionally efficient Y-shaped structure thirty stories in height and containing 3,044 rooms and suites in the three towers that form the Y. The lowest levels and the sprawling grounds around the base of the Y feature public gathering spaces. The exterior is white, counterpointed with reflective gold in horizontal bands that lends it a mirage-like shimmer. The hundred-acre (forty-hectare) property (shared with Treasure Island) includes 2,200 feet (670 meters) of frontage on Las Vegas Boulevard, used to great effect by setting up the resort's Polynesian themes in dramatic fashion, with a volcano and a five-story waterfall tumbling into a lagoon, all visible

The Mirage's Y-shaped main building rose on the Las Vegas Strip at the close of the 1980s, ushering in a new era of fantasy-based mega-resorts. The waterfalls, erupting volcano, lagoons, and tropical plantings offer passersby a crowd-pleasing visual spectacle.

from the street and sidewalk. Throughout the property, gardens, waterfalls, rainforests, birds, flowers, and exotic animal habitats enlarge on the South Seas motif announced by the volcano, which spews fire and smoke skyward every few minutes. As arriving guests leave the Strip, they enter the Mirage fantasy, passing through a lush entry garden amid waterfalls. Drivers arrive via a porte cochère with louvered shutters, evoking a government house from the colonial era.

The atrium lobby offers guests a verdant maze of waterfalls and pools meandering amid a forest of sixty-foot (eighteen-meter) palms, banana trees, orchids, and myriad tropical flowers, all misted by a computerized system and bathed in daylight. Bamboo structures, thatched ceilings, and rattan lobby furnishings enhance the jungle mood. An enormous aquarium behind the reception desk adds to the tropical ambience, its artificial coral reef teeming with sharks, puffer fish, and angelfish.

Nourished by this combination of verdant greenery and South Seas fantasy, the exotic ambience envelops the entire property.

[left, both images] A computerized misting system keeps the Mirage's lobby rainforest lushly appealing. This verdant jungle scene lies just a few steps away from the reception desk, where colonial/South Seas–style furnishings and finishes, including light fixtures, planters, ceilings, carpets, and especially the aquarium behind the reception desk, enhance the fantastic, tropical effect.

[right] The Mirage provides shelter for a number of exotic, endangered species, like tigers and Atlantic bottlenose dolphins, which in turn provide entertainment for resort guests.

Beyond the themed design of myriad food and shopping options and the indoor plantings, the hotel's casino resembles a Polynesian village, with canopied gaming areas scaling down the oversized space. The free-form pool has been sculpted into a series of lagoons, inlets, islands, and waterfalls reminiscent of a South Seas atoll. Siegfried & Roy's Secret Garden provides habitat for rare breeds including white lions of Timbavati, royal white tigers, Bengali tigers, an Asian elephant, a panther, and a snow leopard. The Dolphin Habitat shelters eight Atlantic bottlenose dolphins.

The combination of intense theming, rare and exotic animals in captivity, vastness of scale, and over-the-top, stage-set design is clearly not for everyone. However, for those who take pleasure in these make-believe worlds unto themselves, the Mirage is a revelation, the first and still among the most popular of the new "destination" casino resorts.

•   •   •

From the South Seas idyll of the Mirage, move next door to Treasure Island, courtesy of Robert Louis Stevenson by way of Steve Wynn, who seemingly learned his lessons from Cecil B. DeMille and Walt Disney. In place of a tropical lagoon, imagine Buccaneer Bay, traversed by Las Vegas Boulevard, magically extended over the water in the form of a long wooden dock. The Mirage's erupting volcano has been supplanted by a lively confrontation between the pirate ship *Hispaniola* and *HMS Britannia*, representing her majesty's royal navy. Catching the pirates in the act of unloading their booty, the British call for surrender; the pirates refuse. The battle is joined! Every day, with crowds of tourists watching, cannonballs fly until the pirates win the battle, sending the *Britannia* to the depths of Davy Jones's locker.

Stepping back for a moment, one can see that Buccaneer Bay and the pirate village behind it rest at the base of the hotel building. Linked by monorail to its sister the Mirage, Treasure Island is also constructed in a Y shape, its three, thirty-six-story towers containing a total of 2,891 rooms and suites. Their exterior windows—framed by shutters and balcony balustrades—create a sense of visual unity and hint at the residential mode of the guest rooms within. The

The signage straightforwardly evokes the pirate theme.

pirate theme so theatrically established with the daily battles in Buccaneer Bay extends through much of the hotel's public space. Directly behind the Bay, Buccaneer Village offers a vision of a busy eighteenth-century pirate village, complete with antiqued versions of commercial enterprises typical of the time: foundry, warehouse, sail repair shop, etc.

The source of the fantasy is Robert Louis Stevenson's *Treasure Island*, itself a fantasy of the pirate's life, so why not make it fantastic? Excepting time spent in the quiet of their rooms or in areas where another theme or motif takes precedence, at Treasure Island guests experience the pirate fantasy almost constantly.

Located next door to the Mirage on the Las Vegas Strip and featuring a similar Y-shaped structure, Treasure Island presents guests and passersby with a different fantasy: a full-scale, acrobatic, and pyrotechnically enhanced battle between ships and sailors of her majesty's navy and a ship full of pirates.

[left] The Buccaneer Bay Club overlooks Buccaneer Bay and its battles, along with the Strip. The decor evokes a eighteenth-century colonial dining room, with wrought iron, chandeliers, and other rather rich-looking finishes and furnishings.

NEW YORK-NEW YORK HOTEL AND CASINO

Architecture by Gaskin and Bezanski
Interior design and conceptual planning by Yates, Silverman
Photography copyright New York-New York Hotel and Casino

The Art Deco richness of the interior becomes evident immediately upon entry, as guests arrive at the voluptuously detailed wood-and-bronze reception counter, crowned with a diorama of the Manhattan skyline.

The Las Vegas incarnation of New York City and its world-famous skyline represents the ultimate in entertainment architecture—a fantasy vision of the Big Apple, complete with everything the visitor to New York might desire, except the unruly, unpredictable urban energy of the city itself. Instead, in the sunny neon embrace of Vegas, visitors to the New York-New York experience a tidier, more compact version of the city, decked out with downsized yet realistically detailed recreations of memorable New York landmarks such as the Brooklyn Bridge and the Statue of Liberty. Throughout the 20-acre (8-hectare) property and its nearly 300,000 square feet (28,000 square meters) of public space, including an 84,000-square-foot (8,000-square-meter) casino, design motifs evoke New York icons—Greenwich Village,

Times Square, Rockefeller Center, Central Park, Park Avenue, Coney Island, and Wall Street. Cafes and restaurants feature New York themes and menus. A roller coaster designed after the Coney Island Cyclone weaves through the property at speeds up to 67 mph (107 kph). And rising glamourously above it all to strike a Manhattan pose on the Vegas skyline, the resort's twelve linked towers, each modeled after a famous New York high-rise, contain more than two thousand Art Deco–styled hotel rooms and suites.

The tallest tower, fittingly, is the Empire State Building. Though the 529-foot (161-meter) forty-seven-story Vegas version of the "Emp" is considerably smaller than the real thing, it currently reigns as the tallest hotel/casino in Nevada. Ranging in height from twenty-six to forty-one stories, the eleven other high-rises that shape the hotel's unmistakably Manhattanesque skyline include lovingly detailed replicas of the Century Building, the Seagram's Building, 55 Water Tower, the Lever House Soap Company, the Municipal Building, the AT&T Building, the Chrysler Building, the

[left] The Statue of Liberty, New York Harbor, a fireboat spraying water, Ellis Island, and the Chrysler and Empire State Buildings: New York icons, served up under a flawless Las Vegas sky.

[right] At New York-New York, the wedding chapel is designed as an Art Deco penthouse overlooking Central Park, with a set of perfectly scaled photomurals in the "windows" providing amazingly realistic "views" across the park.

CBS Building, and the New Yorker Hotel. Although the "Emp" rises highest, there is no central, dominant structure and so, no central elevator bank. Instead, the twelve towers are spaced so that guests in one can look out their windows and see others, like in the "real" New York City. In achieving this spacing, the architects put in four separate elevator banks, which in turn generated complicated circulation patterns on the reception level. The designers solved the problem by installing color-coded ribbons in the floor to direct guests to the appropriate elevators.

This make-believe Manhattan comes courtesy of the resort's owners, Primadonna Resorts and MGM Grand. According to architect Joyce Orias, whose firm Yates, Silverman was responsible for conceptual planning and interior design, the idea originated with Gary Primm, CEO of Primadonna. He handed his New-York-in-Vegas notion over to Yates, Silverman, with the request that they base their interior designs primarily on 1930s and 1940s style. Yates, Silverman's Larry Rafferty happened to be a Manhattan building aficionado; and so, between his knowledge (he chose the buildings to be copied for the guest room towers) and several trips east to immerse themselves in the atmosphere of the Big Apple, the designers, architects, graphic designers, and signage planners assembled their own $460 million version of the "city that never sleeps" at the corner of Tropicana and Las Vegas Boulevards.

Generally speaking, the designers' sense of the importance of realism makes New York-New York work. On one level, architect Neal Gaskin recognizes the project for what it is, having referred to it as "one of the largest pieces of pop art in the world." And yet he also understood, as did all the designers, that the look had to be authentic. Because the designers honored the creation of their fantasy by grounding it in believable reality, these buildings entertain with panache. The obvious criticisms of such buildings—lack of originality, history, depth, and "meaning"—are meaningless in the context of Las Vegas, where fantastic structures from differing centuries, cultures, nations, even planets, fight for the attention of fickle gamesters and vacationers. New York-New York uses faux architecture to get the attention of the crowd, but this faux architecture has been built with scrupulous respect for the real thing, providing entertainment at its architectural best.

With a row of brightly colored guest room towers gracefully looming overhead, the spacious, free-form outdoor pool beckons for those who've had enough of the casino. The passage from casino to pool is a wood-paneled promenade with Art Deco ocean liner motifs.

With or without fireworks, the New York skyline transplanted to Las Vegas makes an immediate, dramatic impression, richly enhanced by the small-scale but realistically detailed Statue of Liberty.

[left] The Manhattan Express roller coaster, designed after the famed Coney Island Cyclone, weaves through the property at speeds up to 67 mph (107 kph) and features a 180-degree "heartline" twist-and-dive maneuver; it is only the second roller coaster in the world to have one.

SUNSET STATION
HOTEL AND CASINO

Architecture and interior design by Morris and Brown
Photography by Marc Reynolds

The world on the back of Atlas and the zodiac and stars overhead signal the location of the buffet offering foods from around the world.

Though the heart of Las Vegas still beats along the neon artery of the fabulous Strip, in the 1990s the city beyond the Strip has boomed, spreading into the desert in every direction with endless waves of residential subdivisions. Las Vegas is said to be the fastest-growing city in America, and flying over or driving through, it is easy to believe: the blocks of brand-new, densely packed homes and townhouses seem to go on forever.

Not surprisingly, at least a few casino operators have ridden the residential tide to the edge of town: several casino complexes have been built in the new Vegas suburbs miles from the Strip, where a good portion of the business comes from locals on shopping/gambling trips rather than vacationing tourists. One such outpost is Sunset Station, a major complex designed by the Las Vegas

firm of Morris and Brown. Sunset Station is the latest in a nationwide line of casinos developed by Frank Fertitta III's Station Casinos Inc., with architecture that has been inspired by railroad stations of the Victorian era. Though Sunset Station's design actually derives from elsewhere—the architecture of Spain and Mediterranean Europe—it has a few railroad elements. More importantly, like the other Station casinos, its suburban location had serious implications in terms of planning. Many patrons are area residents on short visits, creating the need for more accessible parking and simpler circulation patterns; these short-term visitors also require restaurants in closer proximity to gaming areas.

Beyond the functional elements, however, lies the design inspiration, and Spain, with its wealth of Moorish influences still intact, proves to be an inspired source for design ideas. Sunset Station offers visitors—guests, gamblers, and gawkers—a rich visual feast. Initially, the sight of this turreted, towered, domed, and lavishly detailed Iberian extravaganza rising out of the shimmering

[left] The Gaudi Bar's gorgeous ceiling reigns over the heart of the casino.

[right] The Sunset Station casino lies in the midst of a vast sea of parking spaces, with a shopping mall (not shown) close by. The hotel's one built wing and three as yet unbuilt wings can be seen at the far right of the building.

23

sea of a suburban parking lot can only be described as surrealistic; but then, after having experienced Egypt, New York, King Arthur's Castle, the tropics, and ancient Rome minutes away on the Strip, the sight of Sunset Station is easily absorbed. It's another Las Vegas fantasy environment. The question becomes, "How well is the fantasy executed?"

At Sunset Station, the architects have done a convincing job, lovingly replicating Spain right down to the details in the tiling. To attain this level of accuracy, at the urging of the owner, the team from Morris and Brown went to the source, traveling to Spain to experience firsthand the Moorish and Old World buildings of Seville and Madrid. As becomes evident when one reaches the Gaudi Bar, located in the heart of the casino, the designers also visited Barcelona, where most of the major works of one of the twentieth century's most original architects, Antonio Gaudi, can be found. Here, it is strikingly clear that the architects paid attention to their sources: this swirling,

multi-colored, voluptuously curving bar could have been designed by Gaudi himself. The architectural reproduction is first-rate.

For the legions of Americans who will never visit Barcelona or any other part of Spain but will visit Las Vegas, a trip to Sunset Station provides a chance to experience a miniaturized, sanitized Spain. The Gaudi Bar may not be the real thing, but it is an honorably executed homage. The same can be said for the Spanish restaurant, the Italian beach cafe, the Greek seafood restaurant, and the race and sports book, inspired by the bull ring in Seville. Painted in romantic sunset tones over the silhouetted turrets and domes of the enchanting Moorish/Spanish structures that wrap around the casino floor, even the sky looks convincing.

Details such as this railing owe their inspiration to the wildly imaginative works of Gaudi.

Perhaps the most architecturally compelling space in Sunset Station is the Gaudi Bar, a masterpiece of architectural homage to Barcelona's greatest architect, Antonio Gaudi. Its changing appearance can be seen in day view [above] and night view [below].

Exteriors show the richly detailed, turreted and towered facade, a Spanish/Moorish extravaganza rising out of a parking lot in the Las Vegas suburbs.

The Station's Spanish restaurant is an original design, but once again, details including artifacts, architectural forms, finishes, and other elements add up to an uncannily accurate re-creation of an elegant Old World dining room.

The architects designed the Capri after a cafe seen by the casino owner on the isle of Capri, off the coast of Italy. The close proximity of restaurants to gaming areas reflects this casino's suburban, local-oriented approach, where everything is just a few steps away to make short trips easier.

THE DESERT INN
RESORT AND CASINO

Architecture and interior design by The Paul Steelman Companies
and Hirsch Bedner Associates
Photography copyright Robert Miller, 1997

Seen across Las Vegas Boulevard, aka the Strip, the 715-room renovated and expanded Desert Inn evokes the Mediterranean-style architecture of classic resort towns like Palm Beach. The main entrance and lobby lie behind the port cochère, left of center.

Amid the heavily themed mega-resorts that line the stretch of Las Vegas Boulevard comprising the Strip, the 715-room Desert Inn stands out as something of a throwback to the early days of Vegas, when most of the hotels offered desert themes, their designs tackily or elegantly evoking the idea of Vegas as oasis or tropical resort. The "DI," as it is rather fondly called by locals by its two letters—literally pronounced "dee eye"—has been completely renovated along those same tried-and-true thematic lines, in a joint venture involving two design firms—the Paul Steelman Companies from Vegas, and the Los Angeles based Hirsch Bedner Associates. The designers have re-created the DI as a modern oasis, with an informal yet elegant look that recalls the classic, casually upscale resorts that once ruled Vegas. With a twist: the relaxed chic of the Desert Inn also evokes that other famed American "oasis," Palm Beach and the Florida luxe architecture of Addison Mizner. Of course, possessing the Strip's only golf course helps lend the DI its decidedly upscale ambience.

The grand entrance lobby in particular reflects Palm Beach high style circa 1930: the lobby atrium rises seven stories above the polished marble floors, with generous expanses of glass revealing the inviting blues and greens of swimming pools and fairways situated just beyond the hotel. In homage to the classics of Palm Beach, the lobby's architectural detailing reflects the same Spanish/Moorish Mediterranean style that came to be associated with that posh Florida community. Hand-painted murals measuring thirty feet (ten meters) high preside over the granite reception counter and evoke the same period, their leafy details lending a whimsical counterpoint to the grandly scaled space and the heroically posed figures in the murals. With an ornately tiled carved granite fountain as

[left] A view from the terrace of the Casa Grande penthouse; the pool goes with Casa Flora, one of the Inn's custom-designed high-roller suites. The Inn's golf course lies directly behind the hotel.

[right] Master site plan

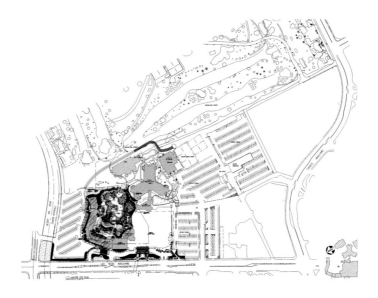

focal point, the lobby sets the elegant yet informal tone that is carried through the entire property.

The resort's 715 guest rooms are housed in five separate buildings. They range from 400-square-foot (37-square-meter) standard double rooms up through superior rooms, mini-suites, and penthouse suites scaled from 1,530–4,000 square feet (142–370 square meters). Upholding the Las Vegas tradition of housing the highest of the high rollers in luxurious accommodations, there are also a number of opulent duplex and multi-room suites with floor plans up to 9,300 square feet (860 square meters) in size, complete with private workout rooms, patios with hot tubs, dining rooms, entertainment centers, and swimming pools.

The hotel boasts four restaurants: the Monte Carlo's four-star meals are presented in an environment meant to evoke the Cote d'Azur, while the Portofino recalls Italian cafes. Both of these high-end dining rooms

overlook the casino from the mezzanine, accessed via a grand stair sweeping up from the main level. The Chinese restaurant Ho Wan ("good luck") features a striking interior design, with engraved entry doors, an inlaid marble floor, an aquarium built into a maple-paneled wall, and three circular dining spaces under domed ceilings finished in silver leaf. On a less formal note, the Terrace Pointe offers twenty-four-hour service in a dining room with a multi-colored slate entry floor that makes this interior space feel like outdoors—a feeling enhanced by the view of the lagoon adjacent to the hotel's free-form, 14,500-square-foot (1,350-square-meter) swimming pool, the largest in Las Vegas. The hotel also offers 30,000 square feet (2,800 square meters) of meeting space, a 636-seat showroom, a state-of-the-art business center, and a 20,000-square-foot (1,900-square-meter) spa with a menu containing every imaginable therapy, body treatment, and massage. A poolside grill, poolside cabanas, tennis courts, a golf club,

and the resort's eighteen-hole championship golf course complete the package.

All these appealing spaces, places, and playgrounds wrap around the heart of the hotel, which is, naturally—this being Vegas—the casino. Here, the designers have attained a measure of elegance in spite of the electronic clang and glare of the slots, with dome-shaped ceilings hand-painted in blue and gold to create the effect of stars bursting across overhead. Imported crystal chandeliers enhance the posh ambience; and at only 32,000 square feet (3,000 square meters), this casino feels, and is, relatively intimate by contemporary Vegas standards. Along with the usual gaming selections on the main casino floor, which include blackjack, craps, roulette, Pai Gow and Pai Gow Poker, video poker, keno, and myriad slots, the casino includes a private race and sports book furnished with the latest in high-tech display boards and video monitors and comfortably deep leather armchairs for patrons. Just off the main casino, a private salon contains three private baccarat parlors, each provided with a private foyer, rest room, and dining room. Detailed with sculpted iron railings and gold velvet drapes, and softly lit by scones, these luxurious private gaming rooms epitomize the classic luxe ambience that has positioned the Desert Inn as a standard-bearer for an alternative Las Vegas possessed of a timelessly elegant sense of style.

[left] The grand entrance to the high-rollers Casa Grande penthouse suite caters to fabulously wealthy patrons.

[right] The casino at the Desert Inn provides players with a more sophisticated ambience than that found at many of the themed resorts, with elegant chandeliers and ceiling murals providing graceful touches.

[left and above] In Las Vegas, there are always a number of high rollers who pay thousands of dollars a day to stay in private penthouses, villas, and suites such as the two shown here.

[right] The high-rollers casino, complete with private dining room, is finished with the kind of luxurious that lend the Desert Inn its posh, Palm Beach style.

CAESAR'S PALACE TOWER ADDITION

Architecture by Wimberly Allison Tong & Goo/Bergman Walls and Youngblood
Interior design by Wilson and Associates
Theming design by James Adams Design
Landscape by Lifescapes International Inc.
Photography by Peter Malinowski/InSite Architectural Photography

The new Italian gourmet restaurant, Terrazza, seats 220 for interior and *alfresco* poolside dining. Pediments, pilasters, and patterns extend the Greco-Roman look.

An established institution on the Las Vegas Strip, Caesar's Palace embodies and celebrates what might be described as the "toga party for adults" concept of resort fantasy. The theme is ancient Rome, the Empire at the height of its power and glory, and all the sybaritic, sensual excess implied by that. The motifs range from the Corinthian capitals and columned, pedimented facades of classical Greco-Roman architecture to the muscular, body-worshipping statuary of the same period. This seemingly is a perfect fantasy for a casino resort environment, lending the dignity of rich historical association to the enterprise and providing designers and architects with plenty of familiar archetypal material to work with.

Recently, Caesar's underwent an expansion and renovation intended to bring it into the competitive new era of Las Vegas mega-resorts. The expansion's primary element is a new twenty-nine-story Caesar's Tower housing 1,134 guest rooms and suites on floors 5–29, bringing the resort's total room count up to 2,471.

On the first four floors, the Tower contains 110,000 square feet (10,200 square meters) of new ballroom and meeting room space, a 22,000-square-foot (2,050-square-meter) spa, a 6,500-square-foot (600-square-meter) fitness facility, and a new business center.

Outside the new building, the designers have created the 4.5-acre (1.8-hectare) Garden of the Gods, a recreation complex including 22,000 square feet (2,050 square meters) of swimming pools. The Garden of the Gods features an oversize circular pool surrounded by fluted, classically scaled columns, marble-lined pools, landscaped gardens of exotic shrubbery and tropical plantings, and a range of classical statuary. With numerous water features and fountains, and a gazebo and reception area for poolside weddings, the Garden of the Gods attains a kind of lavish, over-the-top excess that sends it into the highest ranks of Vegas fantasy resorts. So much marble! So many

[left] The new twenty-nine-story Caesar's Tower addition to the Caesar's Palace throws a Roman facade high above the Las Vegas Strip, with a central pediment featuring a gold leaf profile of Caesar, framed by a gold leaf laurel wreath.

[right] The Roman architecture motifs extend deeply throughout the property, as is evident in this view of one of the many swimming pools.

statues! One expects Cleopatra, as played by Elizabeth Taylor, to appear at any second, preferably carried on a litter hefted by a troop of muscular movie slaves.

The $600 million expansion also added three new restaurants, each with its own distinct design theme; a new wing of the upscale Forum Shops; and a casino expansion of 12,200 square feet (1,130 square meters), containing 151 new slot machines in the Court of Fountains and 125 new slots in the area that formerly housed the Cafe Roma restaurant. Here, and throughout the vast, intricately planned complex, the predominant theme is Imperial Rome in all its glory, reinvented for well-heeled armies of tourists, gamblers, and shoppers descending on late twentieth-century Las Vegas.

The Tower's upscale atmosphere extends into the guest rooms as well. With five different floor plans, they range in size from 550–750 square feet (51–70 square meters). Along with contemporary amenities, every room features a panoramic view, a whirlpool bathtub, 9-foot (2.7-meter) ceilings, and furnishings decorated with ancient coin patterns, Greek key designs, and Pompeii-inspired murals. The theming is evident, but subtle rather than overwrought, thanks to the work of the designers from Wilson and Associates. Stepping back for a moment to view the new tower from afar, one can savor the classical qualities that the architects have added to the tall, rather shallow guest room tower to lend it period

quality. The exterior is finished with fluted columns capped with Corinthian capitals; on top, a trio of dramatic pediments definitively establishes the Greco-Roman credentials. The look is somewhat strange, evoking a kind of vertically elongated temple facade with relatively little volume behind it, but the proportions of the facade appear to have been scaled as correctly as was possible, given the need to make the building twenty-nine stories high. Both outside and inside, though it may not meet the requirements of classical architecture in the most serious sense, the project represents an expansive commitment to neo-classical design in three dimensions. The designers have succeeded in creating an elaborate, entertaining, and very expensive fantasy.

Warm and brightly lit, and decorated with a mix of colorful modern paintings, the high-ceilinged airy Terrazza Restaurant feels contemporary, but the elaborate lighting fixtures and classical architectural elements add a sense of traditionalism to the interior.

[far right] The elevator lobbies illustrate the lavishness of the interior finishes and show applications of neo-classical elements.

The Terrazza offers a mix of indoor and outdoor seating areas overlooking the hotel gardens. The interior has the look of a Tuscan villa, with rustic plaster walls, stone columns and moldings, and aged ceiling beams.

[right] The Roman architectural motifs extend deeply throughout the property.

Harrah's High Limits Casino and Lounge

Architecture and interior design by Creative Resource Associates
Photography by Robert Miller

Mahogany-look laminate paneling on the pit stations enhances the rustically luxurious ambience, as do wall murals of regional scenes.

In the fiercely competitive gaming business, casino operators have traditionally employed a variety of strategies to lure players into their properties. One such strategy is the creation of semi-private, high-stakes areas where those willing to play large sums of money without the distractions of amateur gamblers with little knowledge of the various games can go. In the 1990s, an era when gambling increased in popularity, the number of less-informed players has expanded exponentially. And while these hordes of small-stakes players keep the revenue rolling in, now more than ever before operators need to accommodate, and pamper, the more knowledgeable—and often wealthier—high-stakes players as well. The smaller, more elegant high-stakes casinos fulfill that need.

At Harrah's at Lake Tahoe, the owners added a high-limits casino and lounge as part of an ongoing renovation of the entire property. Located on the main floor of the eighteen-story resort hotel and casino, the High Limits Casino and Lounge has been designed by Culver City, California-based Creative Resource Associates (CRA) in an area previously occupied by a coffee shop and a keno parlor. While true to the property's regionally inspired, rough-hewn mountain ambience—the "alpine elegance" of CRA's overall renovation—the 6,500-square-foot (600-square-meter) semi-private casino and lounge takes the elegant western U.S. stylings one step further, establishing an atmosphere of exclusivity that distinguishes the high-limits area from the surrounding "public" casino and adjacent dining rooms and lounges.

A sense of spaciousness is one element that defines luxury. To expand the volume in the high-limits casino, the designers from CRA dropped the floor 18 inches (46 centimeters), and relocated steel structural beams—clad in distressed poplar to enhance the rustic ambience—around

[left] Designed to mimic the look of a rustically luxurious lodge, the high-limits casino lounge features a wood and stone fireplace as a focal point. The furniture is comfortably over-stuffed, with warm lighting, art, and artifacts adding a level of sophistication reminiscent of a luxurious country home.

[right] Summer view of the casino shows the gorgeous woodland that inspired the interiors.

pyramid-shaped ceiling coffers finished in Douglas fir tongue-and-groove boards. The designers then suspended iron and glass chandeliers decorated with cutouts of deer and pine trees to further the feel—and to fill the voids created by the ceiling coffers. Lighting plays an important part in setting the mood, with uplighting providing a feeling of warmth while minimizing glare off the glass slot machine fronts. An invitingly rich palette intensifies the rough-hewn yet luxurious quality of the spaces, with burgundy and deep blue upholstery, yellow-toned wallcoverings atop limestone-based columns, and wall murals of natural scenery of the area establishing the regional context. Even the pit stations in the gaming area tie in to the design, with mahogany-look laminate providing visual consistency and durability.

The thirty-seat High Limits Lounge, reminiscent of a mountain lodge, offers high rollers a comfortably plush, art- and artifact-rich space accessible from both high-limits gaming areas. Silk wallcoverings and custom millwork set the upscale tone, but the most striking elements are the doors, made of etched glass decorated with wrought iron interpretations of aspen branches and leaves. A wood and stone fireplace provides a focal point in the room, with a firescreen decorated with the same wrought iron aspen designs as the entry doors. Expanding the leaf motif, a metal frieze in a leaf design runs beneath intricate cornices that define the edges of ceiling coffers and conceal lighting coves. Spacious, comfortable furnishings finished with fabrics including leather, chenille, and cotton, counterpointed with wood, stone, and iron, enhance the luxurious yet rough-hewn ambience. The project smartly demonstrates an alternative path to creating a luxe atmosphere, using regional motifs rather than the glitzier stylings that tend to dominate down the road in Las Vegas.

[right] Iron and glass chandeliers decorated with deer and pine tree silhouettes gracefully fill the space created by pyramid-shaped ceiling coffers finished in Douglas fir.

[below] The designers sank the floor and moved ceiling beams to expand the volume in this private, high-rollers gaming area. The "wooden" structural beams are actually steel, wrapped with distressed poplar panels to maintain the rough-hewn yet elegant ambience of the interior.

Details celebrate the region's natural riches. The doors to the lounge are etched glass decorated with wrought iron sculpted into the shapes of aspen leaves and branches. The fireplace screen features the same aspen details.

A winter view of Harrah's Lake Tahoe shows the blocky eighteen-story building in its ruggedly gorgeous natural setting. This magnificent setting served as inspiration for the design of the new high-limits casino and lounge.

[left] The lounge presents a warm, wonderfully knit-together space, with myriad elements—richly colored upholstery, artworks, artifacts, and furniture—assembled to evoke rugged luxury.

[right] High rollers, like other gaming enthusiasts, play slots.

LUXOR HOTEL AND CASINO

Architecture by Klai:Juba Architects
Interior design by Dougall Design Associates (Pyramid Renovation) and
Anita Brooks/Charles Gruwell Interior Design Int'l (Deluxe Tower Suites)
Suite and exterior photographs copyright Circus Circus; interiors by
Dougall Design.

The public spaces on the main level—such as the Ra nightclub [above]—illustrate the Egyptian theming that lends the resort its appeal.

Ancient Egypt arrived on the Las Vegas Strip in 1994 when the black glass sheathed Luxor pyramid first opened to general acclaim. With a sphinx and an obelisk out front, the 2,500-room Luxor took the prize for the most audacious fantasy to date. Within the confines of the sleek black pyramid (more futuristic than Egyptian) however, the fantasy proved decidedly unfantastic, as a plan to move guests by boat from reception to elevators never quite got off the ground—or the dock as it were—and the traffic patterns in the convoluted, multi-level lobby in the base of the pyramid proved difficult to decipher. Nevertheless, the property has flourished since opening, and recently the owners, Circus Development, opted for expansion and renovation, with an eye to clarifying the confused space plan.

Thus in addition to expanding the property with a pair of twenty-two-story, ziggurat-style guest room towers, the local firm of Klai:Juba Architects and the California-based firm Dougall Design Associates supervised a complete renovation of the lobby and reception areas. Eliminating the awkwardly sited "canals" and the multiple sets of stairs needed to bridge them, the architects simplified the circulation patterns, satisfying the need for spatial clarity. The design team then enlarged on the Egyptian theme that lends the hotel its singular identity. Research for this design expedition into ancient Egypt consisted of poring through all the books they could find on the topic, according to principal Terry Dougall of Dougall Design.

The results are impressive. Overscale groupings of Egyptian-style faux stone gods, goddesses, pharaohs, and animals now lord over the lobby and a life-size replica of the Temple of Ramses II—the single most "authentic" reproduction in the hotel—marks the casino entrance with thirty-five-foot

[left] The Sphinx and the Pyramid, with ruins and palms, create a compelling Egyptian fantasy.

[right] Rich yet muted colors, custom finishes, and furniture such as the mahogany four-poster bed in the Presidential Suite lend the property's deluxe suites an elegant, glamorous quality.

(eleven-meter) high figures. Architectural features, some gold or brightly colored, others left natural or finished in desert tones, display carved hieroglyphics and stylized surface decorations in the Egyptian mode, further enhancing the theme. Throughout the interior, in restaurants, casino, lobby areas, and in the Ra nightclub, Egyptian imagery holds sway. Created primarily out of a building material made of gypsum reinforced with fiberglass, most of the Egyptian motifs are generalized rather than specific replications, but no matter, the effect works just fine on the level of fantasy entertainment.

On the exterior, the pair of new twenty-two-story towers are anchored in fifty-foot (fifteen-meter) high bases decorated with hieroglyphics narrating the philosophies of ancient Egypt, while thirty-seven-foot (eleven-meter) high columns are finished to look like bundled papyrus in a nod to the Nile. This enormous, three-dimensional cartoon of ancient Egypt holds its own as one of the most entertaining destinations in Las Vegas.

All but a very few of the 1,900 new rooms and suites have been finished in a style that subtly extends the Egyptian motifs. That select few—half a dozen deluxe suites—instead have been designed in a more luxurious upscale residential mode, one that distinguishes these special quarters from the style of the rest of the property. Distinguished by elegantly detailed custom furnishings, expansive volumes under high ceilings, and sophisticated lighting plans, the suites provide an ambience that evokes Las Vegas glamour at its understated best— an appealing counterpoint to the extravagant building that contains them.

Egyptian elements lend dramatic impact to one of the Luxor's dining rooms.

View of the buffet on the main level further illustrates the Egyptian theming.

[left] The exterior bases of the new towers are anchored with reinforced concrete panels decorated with hieroglyphics narrating Egyptian myths; the columns are finished to look like bundles of papyrus.

[left] The Food Court continues the ancient appeal.

[right] A full-size, faux stone replica of the Temple of Pharaoh Ramses II, who died in 1225 B.C., marks the entrance to the casino in the renovated interior of the Luxor pyramid.

[below] Columns and ferns enhance the Luxor Steakhouse and its Egyptian influence.

RIO SUITE HOTEL AND CASINO

Architecture and interior design by Marnell Corrao Associates Ltd.
Photography copyright Marnell Corrao Associates Ltd.

The Rio's stone-finished Wine Cellar Tasting Room houses a $6 million, 65,000-bottle collection of fine wines, including $1 million worth of Chateau d'Yequem, with vintages from every year from 1855 to 1990.

Located a short distance off the Strip, the Rio Suite Hotel and Casino's sleek, black glass surfaces, bold exterior lighting, and design-driven carnival atmosphere mask one of the more shrewdly organized properties in Vegas. The Rio has been pre-planned for expansion, and will be built in phases so that construction minimally interferes with ongoing operations. In planning the Rio, the Las Vegas design-build firm of Marnell Corrao brought years of experience constructing major casino hotels for clients in Las Vegas and elsewhere.

Room counts lend a sense of how the expansion has progressed: the hotel opened with four hundred suites. Today a recently completed freestanding forty-one-story tower called the Masquerade Village complements the original Y-shaped hotel.

Together, the two structures house 2,563 suites, each with a minimum of 600 square feet (56 square meters) of space. Enhanced with sweeping lines of decorative lighting that lend the curving structure the look, at times, of an enormous jukebox, the Masquerade Village's layered rooflines add an Art Deco-esque touch, intensifying the effect of an already powerful new vertical presence on the primarily low-rise off-Strip Vegas skyline.

Complementing the Rio's 120,000-square-foot (11,100-square-meter) main floor casino, recreational facilities include a complete spa and health club, a nearby golf course and golf club, and a tropical lagoon-style pool area containing three pools, three whirlpools, sandy beaches, waterfalls, and beach volleyball courts. In the colorful, non-stop party that is the Masquerade Village, myriad restaurants and entertainment venues and a shopping area mingle on multiple levels along streets paved with two hundred-year-old Tuscan tile, embellishing the open mezzanine-encircled lower levels of the new tower. Along with the nearby original hotel building, this lively new scene

[left] Straight-on view shows the terraced roofline of the new tower, which provides space for exterior decks to go with the rooftop restaurant. It also lends the building a hint of Art Deco styling, as does the jukebox-style lighting on the facade.

[right] Site plan for the Rio project, with the Y-shaped tower—a favorite with casino architects — embracing the pool area with its sand beach and free-form pools. The newer asquerade Village Tower lies at bottom, the high-end suites overlook the pool at right, and the property's showroom and convention center can be found at top, surrounded by a sea of parking spaces.

makes a package that ranks among the city's most popular resorts. In keeping with the decidedly adult style of carnival, the essential fantasy and the motifs and thematic elements that support it here read a little sexier and more grown-up than do some of the other Strip-based family-oriented resorts.

Holding the many parts together, the simple but evocative Rio motif evokes carnival, masquerade, and the whole sexy, sultry, Copacabana Beach ambience—without literally re-creating the city of Rio de Janeiro or any specific South American design. "The new trend in Vegas is to copy cities," notes Jon Sparer, Marnell Corrao architect. "And we were all set to do the same—to go down there and gather ideas and re-create them here. But then we decided to just do the flavors and excitement of Rio without the literal idea. Instead, we do it with bright colors, a party atmosphere, sizzling, sexy food, and people." With that approach in mind, the flashy, hyperkinetic Club Rio— Copacabana Showroom in the early evening, dance club after midnight—quickly emerged as one of Vegas' hottest night spots. And with serious gourmet Anthony Marnell

at the helm of the company, food naturally emerged as a real concern, generating the development of fifteen distinct restaurants and a world-class wine cellar. Every restaurant features a menu inspired by ethnic, regional, or national cookery, and the style of the food in turn drives the design of the spaces, as is evident, for example, in the elegant interiors of Napa, a French country (by way of northern California) gourmet outpost operated by renowned chef Jean-Louis Paladin.

The designers took advantage of the off-Strip location by making all the walls glass, providing guest rooms with floor-to-ceiling panoramic views of the Strip in one direction and the rugged Black Mountain range in the other. A rooftop bar and restaurant called the VooDoo Lounge dishes Creole food and cocktails with outdoor terraces offering even more spectacular city and mountain views. Even the sandy beaches of the tropical lagoon and pool area have been elevated to enhance views of the city. In a bid to lure clientele off the Strip, the Rio offers guests the only all-suite option in town. Designed in a clean,

contemporary style, every suite has a sitting area defined by a crescent-shaped sofa in addition to the usual pair of queen beds or single king bed. In-room refrigerators, safes, and other amenities enhance the appeal.

The architecture of entertainment takes many guises in modern-day Las Vegas. At Rio, thematic design and space planning help institutionalize the idea of an ongoing party. The style enhances the festive ambience. Rio evokes Latin America's liveliest city, home to the world's biggest and wildest annual party, without literally referring to the city except by name.

[right] Entrance to the Fiore Rotisserie and Grille, which offers Mediterranean-influenced gourmet food.

[below] Late at night the Copacabana Showroom transforms into Club Rio, Vegas' liveliest nightclub, with the stage serving as a high-profile dance floor.

MONTE CARLO HOTEL AND CASINO

Interior and conceptual designs by Dougall Design Associates Inc.
Photography copyright Circus Circus

The Beaux Arts mode assumes many guises in the Monte Carlo. Here, three languid ladies linger in a mural over the reception counter, with its elaborately adorned light fixtures on countertop and ceiling. Richly detailed ceiling moldings and reception counter treatments further the effect.

In the early stages of casino planning, along with site selection, programming, and other prosaic tasks, there comes the moment when the predominant design concept, or theme, must be chosen. In Vegas, the designers and their clients (metaphorically) look down the Strip, see what they're competing with, and contemplate the wide range of complementary worlds waiting to be re-created. Then it's a matter of picking a time and place that will provide plentiful opportunities for compelling design, with architectural and decorative motifs that draw attention to the building and the interiors. The design, above and beyond its functional aspects, must entertain. Once a design team commits to a theme, in a sense the rest comes relatively easy.

Designer Terry Dougall has worked on a number of Vegas casino projects, including the Monte Carlo. Rather than turning to the real Monte Carlo and its legendary casino as a source of design inspiration for this project, Dougall borrowed the famous name and all it evokes, and then found his inspiration in another time in France, in the style and era known as the Beaux Arts. Though he describes the somewhat overwrought Beaux Arts period as unpopular among architects, he "happens to love it," he says. When Victorian English taste migrated to France from 1890–1910, it fell under the influence of Greco-Roman classicism, according to Dougall, and became "more feminine." The results are now described as the Beaux Arts style. Dougall loves this voluptuous "reconfigured Victorian" design, with its Baroque flounces and rococo embellishments and romantic filigree and neo-classical frippery. Having first seen it in buildings constructed for a World's Fair in Chicago, and then seeing it again reconstructed at half-scale in a building in Riverside, California, Dougall decided to plug it into Las Vegas.

And so, in 1995, was born the Monte Carlo: with three thousand rooms in a thirty-two-story tower, and the usual array of restaurants, bars, pools, shops, meeting rooms, and other facilities. Judging from what's on display here, the voluptuous energy and romantic excess implied in the Beaux Arts style are ideally suited for the fantasy world of casino architecture.

[left] In the casino, enormous chandeliers serve as focal points, and a kind of garden effect is established with circular, trellis-like ceiling treatments and plants gathered in white neo-classical-style pots.

The Beaux Arts style is evident in the Monte Carlo's voluptuous statuary.

[right] Raw concrete; metal, and brick; exposed ductwork; brewery equipment, and other basic, unadorned materials create a gritty industrial ambience in the hotel's microbrewery—a complete shift in tone from the lobby, casino, and other public areas.

GAMING BOATS *and* TERMINAL PAVILIONS

THE RE-EMERGENCE OF RIVERBOAT GAMBLING

By Paul Keller

In five short years, the cruising riverboat casino industry moved from markets of vast pent-up demand to saturation, evolving from tiny shoestring operations to significant projects now marketing themselves as destination resorts. The rapid growth of the industry and change in the competitive landscape are very much reflected in the design of the projects. Developers, operators, and their individual host communities have had to experiment with this totally new archetype.

Although cruising riverboats first appeared in Iowa, it was the stunning success in 1991 of the tiny Alton Belle Casino (450 gaming positions) in a suburb of St. Louis that launched a frenzy of business interests grappling to get into the market. While the typical Las Vegas project was going for $750 million, the little $5 million Alton Belle I (a remodeled dinner boat and a floating snack stand) had the highest revenues per square foot of any casino in the country. Five states now allow cruising riverboats (Iowa, Missouri, Illinois, Louisiana, and Indiana). Each state sets its own standards, but generally speaking, the industry has evolved with lightning speed. Today the sixth largest casino in the country is a riverboat project located at Station's Casinos Kansas City property.

From a design perspective, the industry has rapidly and repeatedly reinvented itself. Casinos taken out of the context of Las Vegas or Atlantic City lack the critical mass necessary to re-create the sense of visual and sensory overload now associated with big-time casino properties. If you put the Flamingo by itself on a flat piece of prairie, it would obviously lose something. At the same time, architects designing the exteriors of riverboat casino facilities face the challenge of creating the right marketing image without offending the host community's standards. The after-hours architecture of Las Vegas, still perceived in the Midwest as consisting of big signs and architecture devoid of merit, is simply not going to fly. You might say that no one in Las Vegas ever had to worry about offending somebody's sensibilities, and so this was a new problem for designers and developers.

Faced with city councils that often split on the whole gambling issue, and commonly residing in the middle of historic riverside communities, the better projects have now taken on an appearance that says "Sure, we're a casino, but we have good taste." To achieve this, fewer risks are taken with exterior images. There are quite a few Victorian-looking riverboat casino projects attached to oversized paddlewheelers. Occasionally, an American nostalgia theme will show up, as in Harrah's romanticized Kansas City "ballpark" concept.

Since riverboat casino markets have generally not matured to the niche-marketing strategies associated with most Vegas and Atlantic City properties, riverboat casinos make the effort to be all things to all people, with the most successful properties welcoming high rollers, low rollers, and middle-market players. Ameristar (Council Bluffs) and Argosy Riverside (Kansas City), for example, have probably achieved this balance by combining some of the theatrics of the Vegas Strip with the friendliness of downtown Las Vegas.

TRAFFIC CONCERNS

Unlike their Vegas counterparts—whose interiors are designed to keep people milling about—the standard riverboat casino design keeps people focused on getting to the destination quickly (the gaming boat) and getting them into their cars easily at the end of the cruise. In this regard, land-based facilities associated with riverboats differ dramatically in terms of function and design from their Vegas/Atlantic City counterparts. The casino floor in Las Vegas is the central plaza of the property. The patron must find his or her way through the casino to get to a restaurant, a restroom, and often the hotel registration desk. In the cruising riverboat environment, it's the exact opposite. The preboarding area of a riverboat property is the project's central plaza and is always in front of the casino.

Another major distinction of riverboat properties is the vital connection to a marine environment. The Missouri, Mississippi, and Ohio Rivers are subject to seasonal vertical rises of as much as forty feet (twelve meters). This is a daunting

[left] The glass-topped octagonal entry pavilion at Argosy Casino's terminal building in Riverside, Missouri.

Three generations of Argosy boats signify the growth of the gaming ship.

problem when one thinks about engineering a ramp accessible for everyone, including handicapped patrons, that leads to a target that is moving constantly and within such a large range.

A common feature of most cruising riverboat facilities is the space devoted to the various lines that inevitably form as a result of scheduled cruising. There are queues for coat check (inbound and reclaim), admission tickets, chip redemption, and boarding areas for the casino itself.

In riverboat projects, most of the clientele is local, with many visitations per year. Patrons frequently have a set routine based on the cruising schedule. They have their arrival time down to a science and leave little margin for error. So the operator must have a facility that can handle everyone who wants to park their car, check their coat, buy a ticket, and eat in the buffet, while planning to arrive only forty-five minutes prior to departure of the vessel. In most cases, the land-based facilities are over-designed for the gross number of passengers, but the sequential distribution of demand requires the larger spaces.

PARKING PROBLEMS

Even valet design changes in a riverboat casino project. Patrons often cut it so close to departure that valet goes from empty to pure gridlock five minutes prior to departure. While valet staff gets slammed by the incoming patrons, they are also simultaneously bombarded by outbound passengers finishing the previous cruise. If not handled correctly, an amenity like valet can quickly become dissatisfying for patrons.

Some of the larger properties like Argosy Lawrenceburg and Harrah's Kansas City have figured out how to separate inbound from outbound traffic and avoid snarls. Again, the peaks and valleys of demand for services in cruising riverboat projects is a sharp contrast to the typical land-based casino.

Parking garages built for riverboat casinos can literally make or break a project. The cruising requirement can wreak havoc on the self-park customer if he/she finds himself looking for a space while half the garage empties from the last cruise. It's like trying to park in a garage after the ball game ends. Hammond's Empress Casino, for example, had an eleven-story, two-bay garage that would regularly gridlock. They solved the problem by adding speed ramps. The traffic pattern at the Sam's Town garage in Kansas City caused near paralysis on opening day, and the property quickly gained a reputation as a parking nightmare. Even though the rest of the property set new standards for themed riverboat properties, it could not compensate for this shortfall. The Station's Casinos in St. Louis paid through the nose to solve the problem by constructing the equivalent of a four-lane divided highway right through the middle of its four–thousand–car garage. Unfortunately for the operators, expensive enhancements to parking facilities fail to expand the actual market for casino entertainment.

The proliferation of riverboat casinos in saturated markets like St. Louis and Kansas City has turned them into commodities in the eyes of the consumer. Just as every mall has a Limited and a Gap, every casino has

pretty much the same games. So the designers' challenge has been to create a higher level of perceived value. This is done in numerous ways on the casino floor (i.e., adjusting slots payoff percentages, promotions, player rewards clubs, etc.). However, in the land-based preboarding facility, creating value often is a matter of figuring out how to remove the annoyances of a cruising environment. How can we avoid gridlock in valet before the cruise? How can we feed all the last-minute passengers? How can we entertain them if they missed the boat and have to wait in a nearly empty pavilion? How can we move them in and out of these boats and make them feel like individuals and not cattle? These questions are peculiar to riverboat casino design (as opposed to land-based casinos).

In Missouri, some casinos have dealt with customer annoyance with the ins and outs of cruising by literally building a second (often identical) casino, which boards at staggered intervals to the first casino. So-called "double casinos" have maximum wait times of fifteen minutes versus an hour in a single casino. The Harrah's/Players Riverport project in St. Louis operates a "double-double casino" (literally four casinos) so that there is never a wait—one casino is always boarding. The marketing advantages are obvious, but then again, so are the huge additional costs.

In one of the oddest twists of regulation, riverboat casinos in Missouri do not actually cruise anymore. This came about when the operators and the U.S. Coast Guard expressed concerns about the lack of emergency equipment available on the

rivers. Now six of the state's ten casino projects are actually built on barges that have been made (debatably) to look like boats. Sitting in confined basins like giant glorified tub toys, most of these barges have no engines and couldn't cruise even if they wanted to. Still, by state constitutional law, they have to "simulate" or "pretend as if" they are cruising by having scheduled arrival and departure times. Patrons can get off a "simulated cruise" anytime they want, but they can only get on during the stated boarding times. The operators have to play this cruise game even though they are always in dock. Out-of-town visitors who are denied admission to a docked "riverboat" that has no real engine and then are told to wait until the next "pretend" cruise are left to wonder about this strange regulation.

CASINO VESSEL DESIGN

The first casino boats to appear were basically modified dinner boat designs equipped with casino games and little else. They were narrow, cramped, and smoky. The typical first-generation boat had three decks, about 12,000 square feet (1,100 square meters) of casino space, and contained anywhere from 450–1,200 gaming positions. In terms of size and scale, these early boats were much closer to the "historic heritage" of the river than the current vessels.

However, the limited revenue potential of the small boats pushed the operators to add gaming capacity, and by 1994, the second-generation boats were born. These boats still had three decks but expanded to the range of 900–1,400 gaming positions in 25,000–30,000 square feet (2,300–2,800

square meters) of casino floor space. They also started to lose the classic "banana" shape of the earlier boats as length-to-width ratios began to decline. The air quality of the boats greatly improved as well. A few "composite" boats were built that had a towboat strapped to a three-deck barge and were treated on the outside to look like one long boat. However, the interiors remained a challenge because of low ceiling heights necessitated by the fact that the boats were being built on U.S. territory near the Gulf of Mexico and had to cruise under a series of short bridges to reach their final destination.

The ceiling height problem made it virtually impossible to duplicate the feeling of being in a real casino. The Casino Rouge in Baton Rouge, Louisiana, and the Hilton boat in New Orleans broke the first-generation mold by constructing three-deck boats with a central atrium, allowing a greater sense of openness within the casino. The fact that these boats were in Louisiana near the shipyards vs. Missouri or Illinois allowed them to increase ceiling heights because they did not have the bridge-clearance problem. Ameristar's Casino in Council Bluffs managed to creatively overcome the ceiling issue by constructing only two taller decks of casino space instead of three shorter ones.

THE THIRD WAVE WEIGHS ANCHOR

By 1995 the third generation of casino vessels were under construction. These vessels were being built for the Indiana market where there were no capacity restrictions (as in Illinois, where operators can have a maximum of 1,200 positions). Since licenses were limited by state law and competition

therefore restricted, the operators felt more comfortable investing in the larger vessels. The Lake Michigan boats that focus on the Chicago market are contemporary-looking vessels designed specifically for the higher seas and navigational issues associated with the Great Lakes.

Currently, the largest riverboat casino in the world that actually cruises is the *Argosy IV* in Lawrenceburg, Indiana, serving the Cincinnati, Ohio, market. It has about 75,000 square feet (7,000 square meters) of casino floor and is certified by the Coast Guard to carry up to 4,500 people. The boat was built to just barely clear the locks on the Ohio and Mississippi Rivers and had to lower its stacks to clear the bridges. Each of the three casino decks is larger than a football field. The casino size puts this boat in the range of a mid-size Atlantic City property such as Harrah's. Also, developments in vessel design allow for the elimination of many interior firebreaks, giving the casino a more open, Vegas-like feel than earlier boats. Caesar's is now building a boat for the Louisville market that will be even larger than Argosy's, and will set the bar higher once again.

Paul Keller serves as Director of Development and Construction for the Argosy Gaming Company, an Illinois-based company specializing in the development of riverboat gaming projects. Among the firm's major projects on display in this book are the Argosy Casino Terminal Building and Gaming Boat in Riverside, Missouri, and the Argosy Casino Terminal Building and Gaming Boat in Lawrenceburg, Indiana.

SHOWBOAT MARDI GRAS CASINO

Architecture and interior design by The Hillier Group
Photography by Richard Lanega

By day, the porte cochère to the pavilion, the onshore section of the project, provides a powerful focus for an appealing arrival sequence. At night, the illumination program lends a little glamour to the facade and the entry. The structure at right is a parking garage.

In the 1990s, casino planners rediscovered a classic old gaming venue—the ship. Some of the new gaming ships pay homage to the iconic paddlewheel gambling riverboats of the mythic American frontier; others take a more contemporary tack. Either way, the interiors of these floating gaming palaces generally feature flashy, razzle-dazzle finishes and colors. As is true with many of the new land-based casinos, the high-energy atmosphere on these ships reinforces the concept of gambling as slightly naughty but essentially innocent fun. The Showboat Mardi Gras Casino exemplifies this attitude.

Custom-designed floating casinos either cruise the waters of their designated lake or river or sit at wharfside, tethered permanently to the dock. Many are moored next to onshore terminal buildings containing auxiliary spaces—restaurants, lounges, boarding ramps, and the like—designed by the same architects or planners who designed the interiors of the boats, providing a consistent design on both land and water. Such is the case with the Showboat Mardi Gras, located on twenty-seven acres (eleven hectares) of waterfront land and a picturesque harbor on the Indiana shore of Lake Michigan. With the collaboration of Showboat design consultant Robert E. Curtin, AIA, and naval architects Rodney E. Lay and Associates, the boat and the terminal building interiors were designed by a team from the New Jersey–based architects The Hillier Group. The project includes a 385-foot (117-meter) gaming ship containing a 50,000-square-foot (4,600-square-meter) casino with sixty gaming tables and 1,500 slots. On shore, where the Showboat docks between sailings, the pavilion contains restaurants, public areas, and back-of-house space, along with parking for two thousand cars.

The four-deck vessel offers a Mardi Gras parade theme, with each level

[left] Overview of the project, with four-deck gaming ship at left, pavilion at center, and parking garage at right. The body of water is Lake Michigan.

[right] Plans of two of the ship's four decks illustrate distribution of gaming tables and slot machines as well as locations of the cafe, entries, stairs, bars, and other features.

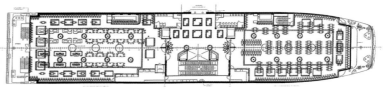

2nd Deck

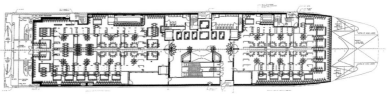

Main Deck

exhibiting a different aspect of the Mardi Gras: the arrival of King Rex, fireworks displays, jesters and parade partying, and the display of jewels and beads that evoke the opulent traditions of the Mardi Gras floats and masked balls. The designers conjure the Mardi Gras atmosphere with brightly colored murals, columns with life-size jesters serving as capitals, enormous jewels, elaborate crowns, star burst chandeliers, and fireworks.

On shore, in the Pavilion's courtyard-like atrium, brightly bannered columns, overscale suspended buntings, and a colorful patterned floor surround a central bandstand designed to resemble a gaudy, multi-hued Mardi Gras float. The bandstand goes up and down, rising into view when the band plays; when the band breaks, the lowered bandstand throws off billowing streamers, displaying bright lights and giant Mardi Gras masks surmounted by dancing jesters. For each sailing of the ship, costumed figures dancing to the music of the live band lead the parade to the boat.

The atrium is ringed with tree-sheltered dining areas. A gourmet restaurant and a VIP lounge and dining room designed as a series of themed environments occupy one side: the lounge features a fireplace and an armory displaying guns and weaponry; the restaurant resembles a grotto-like wine cellar, and a private upstairs lounge, reached via a spiral stair, is stocked with bookshelves to take on the look of a library. From here, VIP patrons overlook the atrium, where the Mardi Gras bandstand sends gamblers on their merry way to the party on the floating casino.

[top] With Mardi Gras-themed murals and colors, the festive atmosphere extends into every section of the pavilion, including the ticketing and promotions area.

[bottom] The entry vestibule on the Kings and Queens deck. Each of the four decks is themed after a different aspect of Mardi Gras.

[right] Escalators lead to the pavilion's central atrium. The carpet, ceiling, and colorful plantings hint at the sensory excitement to come.

The gaming area on the Kings and Queens deck. Brilliantly colored custom carpets, stylized crown column capitals, a highly reflective ceiling, and myriad textures and accessories spilling out, draping down, and otherwise lighting up the room all serve to bathe visitors in a kaleidoscopic wash of intense sensory stimulation.

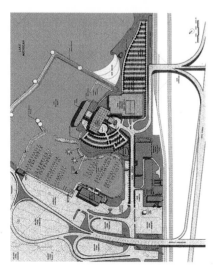

[left] Site plan shows linked ship, pavilion, and parking garage in the twenty-seven-acre (eleven-hectare) waterfront site, with parking lots and marinas surrounding.

The bar on the ship's Jewel deck features bright oversized jewels spilling out overhead and colorful buntings and illuminated trees adding to the festive glow.

[left] The private VIP dining room in the onshore pavilion evokes a grotto-like wine cellar, with stone walls, wine racks, and model ships on display.

ARGOSY CASINO TERMINAL BUILDING AND GAMING BOAT

Architecture by WRS Architects Inc.
Interior design by Anderson/Miller Ltd.
Boat interiors by Interior Design International Inc.
Photography by Mike Sinclair, Sinclair Reinsch Photography

As riverboat gaming laws have evolved over the past few years, the need for dynamic onshore dining and entertainment facilities has become evident, because patrons often have to linger on shore awaiting their turn on the boat, and the boats (or barges) themselves are frequently packed wall-to-wall with gaming tables and slot machines, leaving little room for amenities. Not surprisingly, given the cash-hungry nature of the casino industry, in some cases these onshore auxiliary facilities have become income-generating destinations in their own right. The prosaic ticketing, holding, and waiting functions of a terminal building have been transformed, offering patrons multiple restaurants, lounges, and other diversions in themed environments that can rival Vegas casinos for glamorous, high-impact design.

In Missouri, for example, gaming laws require that casinos float on the water; and so the Argosy Casino's patrons gamble on board a 1,625-passenger faux sidewheeler riverboat afloat on the Missouri River. To entice, entertain, and otherwise divert these patrons awaiting their turn to board the gambling ship, or upon their return from the ship, the Argosy Gaming Company developed the Argosy Casino Terminal Building, an 80,000-square-foot (7,400-square-meter) two-story onshore facility providing riverboat patrons with a selection of dining rooms and other amusements between the parking lot and the casino ship. Employing the history and cultures of the Mediterranean basin as a source of design motifs and colors, planners from WRS Architects Inc., and Anderson/Miller Ltd., crafted an exuberant, richly detailed terminal building as gathering place—a facility that is "an exciting location" in its own right, and "not just an engineered bridge to the boat," according to David Reid, AIA, the project architect from WRS.

The *Argosy IV* holds up to 1,625 patrons, with gambling activities on three levels. Unlike some gaming boats, the *Argosy IV* actually cruises on the Missouri River in the vicinity of Kansas City.

[left] The glass-topped octagonal entry pavilion sets the tone with a dazzling burst of pattern and color, from the central fountain and its surrounding multi-hued sunburst up through tiled planters, exotic palms, and other plantings.

[right] The site plan shows the Argosy Casino Terminal Building with boat, parking lots and garages, and other area features including the man-made harbor on the Missouri River.

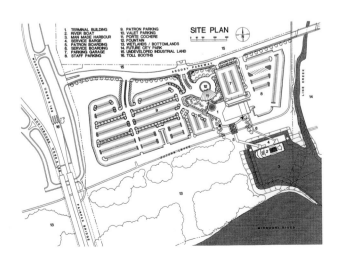

The fantasy begins in transition from parking lot to building, where a series of Teflon-coated, sail-shaped structures fan out from a circular, multi-jet fountain to form a porte cochère. Evoking the spirit of Old World sailing ships, these swooping contemporary forms signal the entry and provide a sense of activity and movement into the Mediterranean-inspired terminal interior.

The octagonal entry lobby packs a powerful punch, with a domed, faceted-glass ceiling and sail-like fiberglass banners overhead; a lavishly tiled fountain centering the room; and vividly colored and patterned mosaic flooring and preserved palm trees and other tropical plantings providing multiple layers of textural and visual excitement, while the glowing dome of the high glass ceiling, its banners lit by multi-colored light fixtures programmed to evoke the feeling of a sunset, serves as a beacon that entices travelers with a warm glow visible from miles away.

From the entry lobby, a passage called the Galleria charts a modified dogleg path to the boarding area. Flanking the Galleria on the ground floor, conveniently positioned ticketing, rest rooms, and coatrooms are followed by a trio of food and beverage outlets. Up and down the length of the Galleria, food carts and openings into the restaurants enhance the visual activity level. At the end of the Galleria, patrons gather at wharfside to board the gaming boat.

With interiors created by a team from the Seattle-based firm of Interior Design International, the gaming boat itself provides another fantasy, three levels of casino dressed up in late Victorian, a period conjured with myriad design elements. On the main or entry level deck, finishes include elaborate hand-painted ceiling moldings, coffered wood panels, and columns crowned with cornucopias, symbols of abundance. Gold and copper embellish the millwork, and custom carpets and tapestries extend the green, copper, and mahogany palette. Upstairs, the second deck evokes a grand Old World ballroom, with crystal chandeliers coupled with special lighting effects to create a dynamic atmosphere. Fine artwork and ornately crafted cabinetry enhance the lavish ambience. On the third deck, the designers created another opulent casino space crowned with a ceiling mural that simulates Tiffany stained glass.

The hybrid form of the onshore pavilion that accompanies the "offshore" gaming boat continues to evolve as developers and designers negotiate the labyrinth of laws that control gambling in these riverfront states, while trying to figure out how to keep their customers happily spending their money. Time will tell how it all ends up; for the moment, projects like this one point in one fairly positive direction, where thoughtful design is not superseded by the superficial values of flash entertainment.

Views of the *Argosy IV* boat interiors reveal a dark, rich design in an elaborate late Victorian mode, enhanced with opulent details, ornate column capitals, and sophisticated lighting.

[right] The entry to Constellations, the pavilion's formal dining room, is decorated with mosaic tile forming a compass on the floor and a curving wall mural of the Mediterranean Basin with a thin layer of water flowing over it.

Visible to the left of the ticket booth, the building's main circulation spine, called the Galleria, leads from the entry lobby past an array of food and beverage outlets to the gaming boat.

[left] The project's circular driveway wraps around a multi-jet fountain, while Teflon-coated sails form a canopy over the porte cochère. The white of the sails and the earth tones of the building exterior provide a dramatic contrast with the exuberant display of ornament and color within.

[right] The white sail forms at the terminal building's entrance maintain the nautical theme.

PORT ARGOSY PAVILION AND GAMING BOAT

Conceptual planning by Argosy Gaming Company
Architecture by American Consulting Engineers, Ratio Architects
Interior design by Designplan, Inc.
Photography by Amy Henning Jobst, Henning Jobst Photography
(except where otherwise noted)

Restaurant interiors evoke different cultures, times, and places including ancient Egypt.

The hybrid form of the riverside terminal pavilion reaches a high point of sorts with the Argosy Casino project on the banks of the Ohio River at Lawrenceburg, Indiana. Accompanied by support facilities, including a six-story parking garage and a three hundred-room Victorian-style hotel, the four-story 186,000-square-foot (17,300-square-meter), Victorian-detailed "world pavilion" offers patrons a selection of food and beverage facilities thematically evoking a diverse array of cultures from ancient Egypt to Renaissance Italy. Remarkably enough, given the lavish nature of the enterprise, the reason for its existence is an adjacent casino floating in a sheltered man-made harbor—a riverboat (and a riverside holding pavilion) connected to the main pavilion by way of an enclosed gangway that spans a levee and has been designed to accommodate up to thirty-five feet (eleven meters) of fluctuation in the river level. Out here in the middle of the country, Argosy Gaming's Paul Keller (Director of Site Development and Construction) and his team of designers and planners—more than twenty firms contributed to the effort—created a multi-cultural fantasy palace. Las Vegas, make room: Lawrenceburg has arrived.

Keller calls the pavilion a "port of adventure," and his conceptual planners have created a fictive narrative to sustain the theme: a century ago, a man named Jonathan Argosy acquired a cluster of Victorian buildings and began modifying and expanding them as he brought treasures from his world travels back to port. These "treasures" now fill the many dining rooms and other public spaces in the building, establishing a fanciful ambience intended to set a tone for the more important business that takes place aboard the gaming boat.

Approached via a four-lane covered porte cochère or by breezeway from the

[left] Inspired by designs found in Moroccan palaces, the centrally located three-story atrium forms the heart of the pavilion. (Photo by Krider Studio)

[right] The site plan shows the main pavilion at center with the hotel directly below it and the gaming boat parked in its own sheltered inlet off the river at far right.

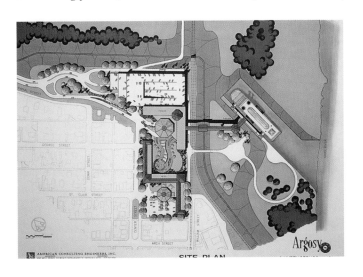

hotel next door, the arrowhead-shaped structure is focused around a central three-story atrium, a dramatic, octagon-shaped volume with a grand staircase, landings, and escalators linking the building's upper levels, where the restaurants and food courts have been located along with the gangway access to the riverside boarding pavilion and the gaming boat. An inlaid compass anchors the atrium floor, while the ceiling is graced with a richly hued stained glass polar map of the world constructed within the largest suspended translucent dome in the United States. Intricately detailed with influences drawn from Moroccan palaces, the colorful, spacious, and light-filled atrium sets the dignified yet adventurous tone that infuses the property.

To make it easy for patrons and employees, the building plan is straightforward. The basement level houses back-of-house facilities. The ground or entry level provides access via the central atrium and its escalators and stairs, and also contains

administrative offices. One level up, visitors discover a dazzling variety of thematically decorated dining rooms: Moroccan, Italian, French, Portuguese, Egyptian, Turkish; there's one designed to evoke the lost continent of Atlantis, while the Moroccan-themed dining room, called Bogart's Grille, owes a debt to *Casablanca*—the movie. Stills of the set for Rick's Bar inspired the decor. Finally, the top level contains ticketing for the boat, coat rooms, a more casual food court, the African-themed Outpost Lounge, and the historic explorer-themed Chart Room Bar and Grill, along with access to the enclosed bridge leading to the riverside pavilion and the gaming boat itself. The dizzying array of decorative styles lends the whole project a kind of theatrical atmosphere—not at all inappropriate for a gaming situation where a sense of stagey glamour is a desirable commodity. Glamour is not traditionally associated with places like Lawrenceburg, Indiana, but the Argosy Gaming Company would like to change

that. As architecture, behind the entertaining decor, the pavilion exhibits a rather prosaic functionalism, and its interiors appear to be somewhat two-dimensional. And yet—they serve their purpose. For the people of this region that serve as the casino's primary client base, the pavilion provides a glamorous fantasy, a place to while away a few hours gambling, steeped in dreams of distant, exotic times and places.

The classical detailing and tilework in the entry illustrate how the designs of Pompeiian Italy inspired one of the dining rooms.

Located on the top floor not far from the gangway bridge, the Chart Room Bar and Grille conjures up a world of exotic travel with tabletop and wall maps, memorabilia, and an old crop duster, 90% intact but repainted to evoke a more adventurous kind of flying. (Photo by Krider Studio)

[left] Inspired by designs found in Moroccan palaces, the centrally located three-story atrium forms the heart of the pavilion.

HARRAH'S SHREVE STAR RIVERBOAT CASINO

Interior design by The Paul Steelman Companies
Photography by Ian Vaughan

The main level presents the "Palace of Fun," a circus-like environment that the designers liken to the mysterious, otherworldly ambience of the Cirque du Soleil. A closer examination of the artworks reveals a sophisticated, entertaining vision of acrobats, clowns, and assorted harlequin figures.

The Paul Steelman Company designs casinos on land and on water, in Nevada, New Jersey, and Mississippi; on Native American lands; and in Europe, Canada, South America, and Africa. They've designed every imaginable style and scale of gaming institution, including a number of riverboats like Harrah's Shreve Star, shown here.

Constructed in Missouri, then moved to Louisiana and moored next to a waterfront pavilion containing an array of restaurants to entertain patrons prior to boarding, the Shreve Star resembles an old-fashioned riverboat in keeping with a Missouri law requiring the traditional look. However, the designers fulfilled the requirements of the law without going to great trouble to give it real period authenticity. Instead, the shape of the boat, woodwork, and painted details are used to simply evoke that old-time look. This works fine for this particular gaming boat, since it doesn't leave the mooring site and most of the passengers are there to gamble, not to check on the authenticity of the boat. In addition, the needs of a modern casino dictated certain non-old-fashioned structural elements, like expanded floor-to-floor heights to accommodate bulky casino equipment. Like most casino boats, Shreve Star was built by a naval architect with the casino designers coming in after the naval architect did the basic floor planning.

The Shreve Star has three gaming floors, each with a different fantasy concept. They are the Palace of Fun, the Crystal Palace, and the Palace of the Universe. As is

[left] The Shreve Star was built in Missouri, where the law requires that the exteriors of riverboat casinos sport nineteenth-century riverboat style.

[right] Second and third deck floor plans

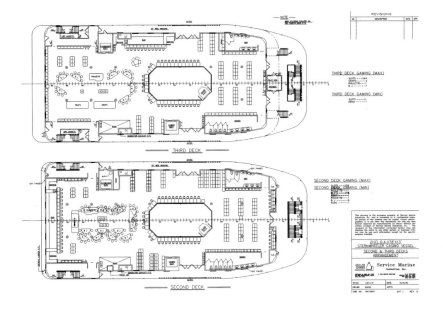

evident from the photos, in each case the designers have worked the volumes rather intensely with colors, forms, and finishes to achieve the desired effects. The main level Palace of Fun, notes Steelman, was inspired by the Cirque du Soleil, and represents "not a circus for kids but rather a magical, mysterious place somewhere between the earth and another reality." The middle level Crystal Palace suggests to patrons that they are inside a glass palace or a nineteenth-century botanical conservatory, perhaps, looking out at a series of spectacular gardens. And the top level Palace of the Universe, Steelman's "only successful blue casino," he says, offers representations of the moon and stars. On each level, these motifs play out in myriad ways, from carpets to walls to columns capitals to ceilings. Though there's a sort of relentlessly high visual volume to the theming, some of the murals and other effects are genuinely lovely. Besides, when what you're dressing up is a room containing banks of noisy electric slot machines and flat green gaming tables, it can't hurt to make the designs as bright and attention-grabbing as possible to sustain an upbeat mood.

Gilt and crystal conjure a rich, old-fashioned ambience.

[below] The middle level "Crystal Palace" level evokes the interior of a nineteenth-century botanical conservatory in a tropical environment, with peacocks, exotic flowers, and other elements in garden-view murals on the walls and ceiling.

[right] Wall murals enhance the genteel 19th century mood the designers sought to establish in the casino.

NATIVE AMERICAN CASINOS

NATIVE AMERICAN CASINO DESIGN

By Paul Steelman

In the early 1990s many Native American tribes negotiated a compact within their state for gambling to be permitted on their sovereign land. The compact led to the creation of a unique entertainment design based on history and culture—a design that was not a museum or cultural exhibit but an interactive, living casino facility.

Native Americans have a colorful and rich history, and in many cases designers are able to use historic and cultural elements in creating themed gaming facilities. Like other design firms working with tribal casino planners, our firm created several Native American casinos employing aspects of tribal history and culture. In doing so we came to recognize that tribal imagery works very well with the excitement and dynamic of casino design, for a number of reasons. With proper lighting, tribal colors and patterns can be integrated into memorable visual experiences. Native American designs do not "date" or wear out. Because of the Native Americans' traditionally close relationship with nature, Native American-based designs connect easily with the exterior environment, allowing the designer to create an exciting inside/outside relationship. Also, Native American imagery often includes unique and compelling graphic elements.

Native American casinos differ in the following ways from standard casinos: Native American sites are suburban. There is no "walk-up traffic." All patrons arrive by automobile. The Native American casinos usually start out small with an extensive, multi-component master plan that extends over a period of years. This approach reflects the fact that most tribes do not have the initial capital investment necessary to construct large projects. When they go into partnerships with gaming companies to obtain expertise and financing, the contracts are usually only valid for seven years, which may not provide enough time to capitalize a large-scale project. Unlike many standard casinos, Native American projects do not usually feature adjacent non-gaming entertaining elements such as theaters or retail complexes. It is difficult for Native Americans to create joint venture partnerships with developers on sovereign (tribal) land, since most developers are non-Native American, and will not accept the judicial systems and laws of the Native American land. Finally, Native Americans generally use the proceeds from gaming operations to improve the lot of the entire tribe—who are in effect joint owners of the properties—rather than just the employees.

Native Americans have taken their rights to gambling to traditionally non-gaming areas and created new multi-disciplined entertainment companies. As their financial situations improve, in the near future many Native American companies will probably construct massive gaming palaces off-reservation that will compete effectively with all of the well-known Las Vegas-based gaming companies.

Paul Steelman is president of The Paul Steelman Companies, a casino design, architecture, and planning firm based in Las Vegas, Nevada. The firm has completed themed casino projects all over the world, including numerous Native American casinos, gaming riverboats, and American-style casinos in France, Switzerland, Peru, and the Philippines.

[left] A view of the interior of Harrah's Skagit Valley that recalls the cheery tones of the oceanside.

stories that serve as a kind of thematic backbone for projects. For the Mohegan Sun, the firm's first casino project, Rockwell looked to the Mohegan tribe itself, meeting with tribal historians and immersing himself in the tribe's culture and lore. Drawing on tribal mythology and iconography, the Rockwell design team developed an architectural vocabulary and a workable space plan for the 200,000-square-foot (19,000-square-meter) casino, a circular volume under forty-five-foot (fourteen-meter) ceilings. Challenging the conventional wisdom on casino design (which says that no one should know where they are or the time of day when gambling), the designers made a floor plan that divides the circular space into quadrants oriented by the four cardinal points of the compass and installed skylights over the cardinal points to let daylight into the interiors; thus casino patrons know day from night and know where they are in the building.

Like virtually everything else in the design, Mohegan mythology inspires the circular plan: the four-quadrant medallion represents life and family in tribal myth. The quadrants also represent the four seasons, creating a link to the natural world—and providing a thematic basis for the casino's four porte cochères, where Mohegan-style log structures guide visitors into seasonally themed entry pavilions. These pavilions link to the main casino areas by a circular path that winds around the entire floor, with a carpet designed to evoke movement along a "life trail" decorated with nine of the thirteen Mohegan moons (the others have been inset in terrazzo in the four entrances). Within the circle contained by this path, banks of slot machines and gaming tables are neatly arrayed around a 10,000-square-foot (930-square-meter) central circular space, called the Wolf Den after the

Mohegans' historic designation as the Wolf People. Enclosed by wood beams and stretched artificial hides, the Wolf Den seats up to 350 for films, live performances, or other events.

Around the perimeter of the round casino floor, more banks of slots and gaming tables occupy two sides, while a third contains a rain forest-themed food court flanked by seven ethnic restaurants. Accessed through the Oyster Terrace, a transitional lounge space, the restaurant offerings range from Chinese to Italian to Wild West to New York delicatessen. Each dining room design matches its menu, with motifs ranging from bamboo forests in the Asian restaurant to screens of woven twigs in the Western-themed Longhorn Cafe.

The standard ceiling height in casinos is generally around fifteen feet (five meters); the Mohegan's unusually expansive forty-five-foot (fourteen-meter) vertical volumes gave the designers the opportunity to create a dazzling sensory extravaganza integrating authentic Mohegan symbols and stories into a dynamic, multi-layered stage set that transforms every patron into a player. The designers installed stretched fake animal hides, totem-like pole structures, overhead truss systems supporting light fixtures, myriad fiberglass trees, and trellis-like structures to break up the voluminous space. Custom carpets, fabric, and wall treatments enrich and deepen the tribal motifs, while real stone partitions and Adirondack-style wood structures lend architectural details from another place and culture, the Adirondack great camps of the nineteenth and early-twentieth centuries. Throughout the project the "fake" mixes comfortably with the "real," establishing a seamless, appealing fantasy based primarily on an imaginative yet respectful interpretation of Mohegan mythology and culture.

[far right] The Asian restaurant offers visitors space for casual, intimate gatherings.

[right] Cane seating, fabric printed with Asian figures, fiberglass bamboo, translucent fabric light screens, and a carpet that mimics the black stones that hold the bamboo all contribute to the bamboo garden-like atmosphere in the Asian restaurant.

and beach-related notions are immediate and obvious. The new building, a pleasant enough structure with small towers and cupolas to make it more visible from a nearby highway, has the look of a typically pseudo-old-fashioned retail structure, as one might find in a tastefully planned outlet center or a small town shopping area. It is relatively understated by day, and then glows with lively exterior lighting at night. The interiors gleam bright and cheery. It all hangs together after a fashion, creating an atmosphere conducive to escape, fantasy, and having fun gambling away an afternoon.

[right and below] Images from the casino's interior illustrate how bright, cheery colors support themes derived from the ocean.

The Harrah's Skagit Valley tribal casino in Skagit Valley, Washington, has the look of a typical new Northwest U.S. building designed to look like it has been around a while, with old-fashioned detailing adding richness, and cupolas and towers lending it higher visibility. The tribe elected to avoid using any of their own cultural imagery or icons in the casino design.

HARRAH'S
AK-CHIN CASINO

Architecture and interior design by The Paul Steelman Companies
Photography by Ian Vaughan

After assisting Harrah's in winning the contract to operate this casino for a local Arizona tribe, The Paul Steelman Companies worked with both tribal representatives and Harrah's to develop the architecture and design. Although the tribe did not want sacred imagery or iconography from their cultural or religious history to be used in the design, they did request that the property evoke the southwest region, and also gave permission to use imagery that reflected their lifestyle and surroundings.

The Southwest's architectural styles evolved from both Native American and Spanish sources. Reflecting this, the designers turned to Spain (and its Moorish influences) for architectural motifs. In fact, according to designer Steve Anderson, it was the brilliantly eccentric Barcelona architect Antonio Gaudi whose imaginative style influenced the exterior look of the building. "The domes and rooflines are from Gaudi," he says. The interior decorations, on the other hand, illustrate and reflect the life of the Native Americans who still live in the area, as they have for thousands of years.

Beyond that, following the preferred Harrah's mode, the slot machines are up front, close to the entrance. To minimize the "warehouse" feeling generated by the sea of slots and tables, the designers shifted ceiling heights and utilized various ceiling treatments to break the space into smaller zones, such as the octagonal room housing the high-end slot machines. The combination of Southwest motifs, bright lights, and lively colors establishes the upbeat, fun-oriented mood the operators sought. It also identifies the tribal essence of the property without exploiting and thus devaluing tribal icons and imagery.

The gaming areas are organized into octagonal spaces beneath central chandeliers and raised ceilings. Each of these spaces is located beneath one of the domes on the roof of the building.

[left] Native American and Southwestern culture is evoked in Ak-Chin's design while still reflecting the tribe's wishes to avoid using its religious icons.

[right] The octagonal hotel and multi-level parking garage facilitate long- and short-term visits.

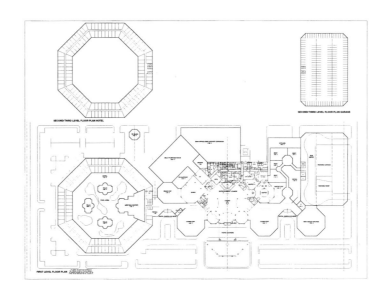

Native American casinos remain a kind of separate entity in the casino universe; with more of them opening and competition heating up, however, they are beginning to demonstrate a more sophisticated approach to design, as is reflected in this entertaining project.

[left and above] Without using specific imagery from the tribe, the design evokes and idealizes Southwestern Native American culture and history with colors, decorative motifs, murals, and even playful items like the metal cut out Native Americans with spears on horseback galloping around the lighting fixture in the buffet area.

CARIBBEAN CASINO RESORTS

WESTIN RIO MAR RESORT AND COUNTRY CLUB

Architecture by Sierra Cardona Ferrer
Interior design by Hirsch Bedner Associates
Photography by Durston Saylor

Like many Caribbean hotels, the Westin Rio Mar contains a casino that serves as a small but integral part of the complete resort package. The casino design essentially extends the motifs and themes that define the style of the entire property, a seven-story, six hundred-room resort and conference center with interiors designed by Hirsch Bedner in close collaboration with the owners, Tishman Realty Corporation and Willowbend Development Corporation. These themes represent an effort to create a "contemporary interpretation of an elegant Caribbean manor house," Hirsch Bedner team leader Holly Kappes says.

Sited dramatically between mountains and sea on the Atlantic coast of Puerto Rico, the resort is anchored by a plant-filled atrium lobby organized around a central fountain, which offers panoramic water views. The Caribbean Spanish architecture of old San Juan inspired the staircases, courtyards, and fountains, while the multicultural mélange of Puerto Rico in general finds expression in differing parts of the hotel designed to reflect myriad national and ethnic influences, with furniture, artworks, rugs, and artifacts from Spanish, French, English, Dutch, and Latin American traditions. Typical local materials like sisal, stone, stucco, and tile hold it all together, and also withstand the heat and humidity of the tropics. The palette reflects natural imagery, especially the lush greens of the nearby El Yunque rainforest, the blues of sea and sky, and the bright bold colors of tropical birds and flowers. Throughout the property, in most of the hotel's public spaces such as the lobby, lounges, and restaurants,

The lobby lounge area is crowned with a dome hand-painted with rainforest plantings and tropical birds.

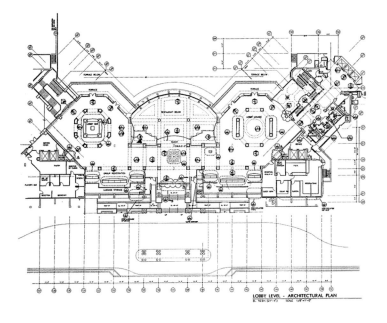

[left] Blues of sky and sea were a primary influence on the color palette; in classic warm weather tropical mode, the resort's public areas spill from interior to exterior. Water features exert a cooling influence.

[right] Main lobby level

LOBBY LEVEL - ARCHITECTURAL PLAN

Scrolled ironwork lends the stairs a traditional feel, balanced with a casual, contemporary sensibility evoked by fabrics and furnishings.

[right] The property's high-end restaurant is called Palio. Marble tiles, elegant pendant light fixtures, classic table settings, and wrought iron details place the interior in the formal European tradition.

the designers and architects utilized arched window openings, doorways, and other elements to frame views of the mountains and the sea.

In the lobby lounge, a hand-painted domed ceiling offers an artistic interpretation of rainforest flora and fauna, while the lobby bar features tent-like striped fabric to simulate a beach cabana. A pair of grand stairs descend from the lobby to the lower level dining rooms. The resort boasts no fewer than eleven distinct restaurants, with the design of each keyed to a different theme.

The six hundred balconied rooms and suites feature a relatively informal style, with island influences evident in the distressed mahogany, sisal floorcoverings, bright fabrics, wrought iron details, and locally produced artworks. The guest rooms reflect the style of the property as a whole: a contemporary interpretation of Caribbean design, enhanced with the casual comforts modern travelers on business or pleasure have come to expect. The vibrant, colorful resort draws its influences from regional sources, and these diverse sources have served it well.

HYATT REGENCY ARUBA

Architecture by Thompson, Ventulett, Stainback and Associates
Interior design by Hirsch Bedner Associates
Photography by Jaime Ardiles-Arce

The design inspiration for the 390-guest room Hyatt Regency, on the beach in Aruba, lies in Latin America, not unsurprisingly since the coast of Venezuela is just 9 miles away from this nearly southernmost of all Caribbean islands. More specifically, the interiors draw on motifs derived from grand, traditionally decorated South American homes, coupled with that ubiquitous, colorful, and festive Latin American party, Carnival, a seemingly inexhaustible source for casino interior decorations.

Tile, stucco, wooden beams, and comfortable, residential-style furnishings and carpets create a casual Old World environment, enhanced with an open-air verandah providing spectacular views out over the island and the water. The lobby also overlooks an area of faux "ancient ruins," the remains of a mythic ancient civilization said to have inhabited the site in some make-believe past. The make-believe doesn't matter; instead, it provides a springboard for a charming fantasy, with ruined rock walls framing water features and other appealing elements.

In the casino, another kind of fantasy takes over, as the exotic, non-stop party of Carnival comes to life via neon re-creations of Carnival costumes, mounted Carnival headdresses, and gold palm leaf capital columns infusing the space with vibrant color. Behind the bar, a colorful mural swings open to reveal a stage with a live band playing salsa, merengue, and other island music styles. This particular evocation of Carnival succeeds in making the sometimes dreary glamour of slots and gaming tables come to life.

The "ruins" provide a thematic basis for one of the resort's two restaurants as

The Cafe Grill is the more casual of the resort's two restaurants. Located on the beach, the cafe's bright colors, wooden construction, and casually assembled interior suggest the laid-back style prevalent in homes and local restaurants all over the islands.

[left] The casino design evokes Carnival, the annual Latin American party that inspires more costumes, revelry, and wild, sensual behavior than any other festival in the world. Specific Carnival elements include mounted headdresses and neon costumes, while a bandstand hidden behind a colorful mural, columns with palm capitals, and glittery, razzle dazzle lighting more generally evoke the Carnival mood.

[right] The ruins of a mythic civilization that once occupied the site create a fantasy archeological setting in the resort's gardens and pool areas.

well. Ruinas del Mar is meant to represent the largest remaining fragment of the ancient lost civilization, evoked with a temple shape, fountain of fire, and man-made waterfalls. The Cafe Grill provides a more typically Caribbean option, with bright colors and comfortable wooden furniture establishing a casual atmosphere in a building located directly on the beach.

Guest rooms partake of the vibrant, verdant Caribbean colors, with an emphasis on greens and fuchsia counterpointed with rubbed bleached wood and other local materials, creating a connection with the local culture—a connection richly enhanced throughout the project with local arts and crafts as well as materials.

[right] With windows designed to maximize views across the Caribbean Sea, guest rooms have been finished with an eclectic, crowded, and casual mix of furniture, fixtures, and artworks that reflects the southern Caribbean region while upholding the standards of comfort and convenience expected by modern travelers.

[below] The lobby offers an appealing mix of residential furnishings, traditionally-styled wrought iron chandeliers, and custom carpets in floral patterns—a comfortable, casual combination that establishes the Old World ambience sought after by the designers.

ATLANTIS RESORT AND CASINO

Architecture by Wimberly Allison Tong & Goo
Interior design by Wilson and Associates
Photography copyright Sun International

The Lazy River Ride provides guests with an opportunity to float "downstream," beginning and ending in the River Pool.

Prior to the arrival on the scene of Sun International, Caribbean resorts seldom strived for Las Vegas scale or Las Vegas–style fantasy. Operators assumed that sun, sea, surf, and all that tranquil tropical beauty was enough. Choose your market and scale to match, build a pretty hotel on a pretty beach, throw in a diverse array of restaurants, lounges, meeting rooms, and perhaps a casino, and the rest would take care of itself. However, when Sun International purchased the Paradise Island Resort and Casino and transformed it into Atlantis, the Caribbean equation changed. Whether Atlantis signals the beginning of a new era of fantasy-driven Caribbean mega-resorts (in the same way the Mirage opened the new era in Vegas) or represents a highly successful, one-of-a-kind event remains to be seen.

Whatever the long-term effect may be, Paradise Island and the Bahamas have been revitalized as a tourist destination by the transformation of the formerly slightly run-down resort. The 1,147-room property has been completely renovated, with a resort-wide master plan and architectural reorganization supplied by the firm of Wimberly Allison Tong & Goo.

The centerpiece of the new Atlantis is the fourteen-acre Waterscape, an elaborate salt- and freshwater amusement park that includes six exhibit lagoons featuring different collections of fish and other sea animals (there are thirteen thousand fish representing a hundred species in the complete collection), forty waterfalls, three swimming pools, two underground grottos for underwater wildlife watching, an underwater pedestrian tube for viewing sharks, and artificial coral reefs designed from casts made at

[left] An aerial overview of Atlantis, with the Waterscape in the foreground and guest room towers to the rear. The round Lagoon Bar lies at right, on the shore of the eight-acre Paradise Lagoon. The real ocean and beach are at far left, with the various swimming areas in foreground center. The low-rise buildings house collections of suites as well as meeting rooms, restaurants, and other public areas.

[right] Drawing of the Atlantis Phase One site shows how elaborate waterscapes, pools, and pathways weave among the guest room buildings, creating a tropical fantasy.

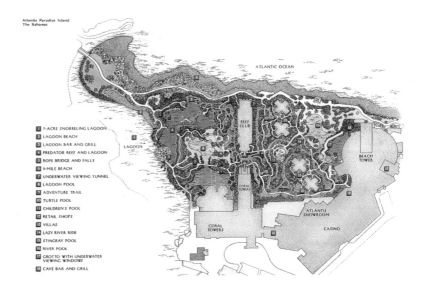

Atlantis Paradise Island
The Bahamas

1 7-ACRE SNORKELING LAGOON
2 LAGOON BEACH
3 LAGOON BAR AND GRILL
4 PREDATOR REEF AND LAGOON
5 ROPE BRIDGE AND FALLS
6 3-MILE BEACH
7 UNDERWATER VIEWING TUNNEL
8 LAGOON POOL
9 ADVENTURE TRAIL
10 TURTLE POOL
11 CHILDREN'S POOL
12 RETAIL SHOPS
13 VILLAS
14 LAZY RIVER RIDE
15 STINGRAY POOL
16 RIVER POOL
17 GROTTO WITH UNDERWATER VIEWING WINDOWS
18 CAVE BAR AND GRILL

authentic reef sites. Assorted swimming pools, slides, river rides, and spa pools provide visitors with more active choices. With four acres of dry-land tropical landscaping interwoven amid the water features, the Waterscape distills the oceanic experience into a safe, accessible "ride" that provides less adventurous tourists with access to sights usually seen only by divers and sea-going adventurers. As Sun International chairman Sol Kerzner said, "What we've done here is enhance reality with an entire universe of experience . . . what used to be only available to scuba divers is now available for the enjoyment of all our guests, and on a scale they can hardly imagine."

The hotel pulls them in as well. A dozen restaurants offer a variety of menu offerings. Throughout the property, renovations have been made with an eye to opening things up, with atriums and skylights providing more daylight and fountains, plantings, sculptures, and sea life motifs extending the aquatic Atlantis theme into an all-embracing environment. The property now features two registration/arrival lobbies and three distinct guest room areas, called Coral Towers, Beach Tower, and the Villas. 100,000 square feet (9,300 square meters) of meeting space includes two ballrooms and eighteen meeting rooms. The Atlantic Showroom provides seating for up to a thousand people for Vegas-style shows.

With 30,000 square feet (2,800 square meters) of floor space and 826 slot machines, the Paradise Island Casino is the largest in the Caribbean. Located between the two main lobbies, the casino's design, from top to bottom, reflects the aquatic themes that rule the resort, with fiber optic nautical signage highlighting the slots areas and the sixty-five gaming tables.

Currently under construction, the Atlantic Resort's Phase Two adds 1,208 lavish guest rooms and suites in new Royal Tower buildings. The expansion will also see the opening of another 100,000-square-foot casino, along with a Mayan Temple, several new restaurants, new water features, and other entertainments. Also part of the plan is a fully developed narrative myth centered around an invented archaeological excavation, "The Dig," which sets out to establish that this resort is indeed the long lost kingdom, or continent, of Atlantis.

[right] One of twelve restaurants on the property, Seagrapes features a design inspired by the marketplace, and serves tropical food from around the world, with an emphasis on Cuban, Cajun, and Caribbean menus.

[below] The Lagoon bar ceiling and stairway expands on the Atlantis theme with painted fish as well as cast metal dolphins, coral forms, shells, and other oceanic elements.

The Reef Club is a separate wing within the resort, with ninety-two luxurious rooms offering guests a higher level of service than standard rooms.

[below] Among other things Atlantis Phase Two will bring a life-sized replica of a Mayan temple to the property.

One of the more spectacular attractions at Atlantis is a long pedestrian viewing tunnel that allows guests close-up views of sharks, barracuda, and other denizens of the Predator Lagoon.

[left] The Lazy River Ride offers guests a quarter-mile float down a man-made river.

EL SAN JUAN HOTEL AND CASINO

Interior design renovations by Jorge Rossello
Casino and Royal Suite Photography by Robert Cerri
Other photography copyright El San Juan Hotel

Shown is the Palm Court Lobby and its famous oval bar and oval-shaped crystal chandelier. The columns and ceiling are crafted of carved mahogany, while the walls and floors are finished in rose marble taken from a single quarry in Italy.

Upon opening in 1958, El San Juan Hotel and Casino quickly emerged as the exemplar of Caribbean style, combining sophisticated urbanity with the tranquil appeal of a beachfront resort. After the party that was Havana shut down with the Cuban Communist Revolution, for a time the Spanish colonial-tinged El San Juan stood out as the one place in the Caribbean that reminded travelers of Havana in its heyday.

Then hard times hit, and the hotel endured a stretch of bankruptcy and near ruin in the early 1980s. The first renovation and re-opening, supervised by San Juan's Williams Hospitality Group, took place in the mid-1980s, after Williams, the only party bidding, bought the place at a fire-sale price. The hotel has done well in the years since, and in light of that, and in an effort to stay ahead of the trend curve, a second renovation has just been completed. Today, after three years and $72 million in renovations masterminded by the Puerto Rican artist-turned-designer Jorge Rossello, the El San Juan has re-established itself as the crème de la crème of Caribbean hotels, home to the most elegant casino west of Monte Carlo and several of the finest restaurants south of Miami. And the newly refurnished Palm Court lobby still ranks among the most lavishly enticing hotel lobbies in the world.

In describing the interiors, one should begin with that lobby and its vaulted, intricately carved mahogany ceiling and columns. Beneath, the walls and floors are finished in rose marble, all taken from the same quarry in Italy. Along with a completely new array of furnishings, existing lobby artworks and accessories include nineteenth-century French landscapes,

[left and right] Whether playing for high stakes in Private Players high roller areas or for low stakes on the main casino floor, guests at the El San Juan find a recently renovated casino that has lost none of its Old World grace and sophistication. Crystal chandeliers, richly carved mahogany ceiling coffers, gold leaf finishes, and myriad elegantly styled light fixtures all contribute to the glittery glow of "James Bond" ambience—and that reference is grounded in reality: 007 movie casino scenes have been shot here several times.

Italian sculptures, Art Deco lamps, and Oriental vases. Over the lobby's oval-shaped bar, an enormous, oval-shaped, hand-cut Czech crystal chandelier glitters invitingly, helping create a surprising sense of intimacy in the very spacious lobby. Other lobby spots—there are nine socializing venues— include a French bistro, a wine bar, and a new cigar bar featuring a custom-designed ventilation system and computer-controlled humidifiers. The hotel's nightclubs include El Chaco, styled after a Spanish saloon of the late nineteenth century, and the Club Babylon disco.

Adjoining the lobby, the El San Juan's richly decorated casino represents the ulti-mate in sophistication and style—as is

evident in that it has been featured in numerous movies, including several James Bond films. The 16,500-square-foot (1,500-square-meter) gaming room was expanded in the recent renovation to make room for a lounge with a performance stage close to the action, a VIP slots area, and the new Private Players (high rollers) "Crystal Room." The refurbished casino features dark mahogany paneling, gold and red fabrics, and elaborate chandeliers along with newly upholstered casino furniture and new lounge furniture.

The hotel's nine restaurants offer a wide range of ethnic cuisines, including a new branch of the Palm, New York's grand old steakhouse and The Ranch at El San

Juan, a rooftop dining room (facing the hotel's much-loved Tequila Bar and Grill) featuring American country-and-western dining and music—surely a first for Puerto Rico. Among the other restaurants, the nuevo Latin dining room, called Aquarela (watercolor), has garnered the most atten-tion for its lively interiors as well as the styl-ishly trendy food created by rising star chef Douglas Rodriguez.

With the total room count projected to end up at 509, the hotel's rooms and suites have been completely refurbished, and twenty-one lavishly furnished ocean suites have been added in a new two-story wing located directly in front of the hotel's seven hundred feet (two hundred meters) of white sand beach. The epitome of luxury is reached in the Royal Suite, furnished with antiques and case goods with inlaid black lacquer, Limoges china, and Baccarat crystal glassware. The suite was originally fur-nished to meet the posh requirements of a regular guest, who has since departed for another part of the world. The hotel pur-chased the furnishings and left the elegant suite completely intact.

Several pools and whirlpools, a shop-ping arcade, watersports rentals, and a rooftop spa complete the package, which comes wrapped in eight acres of landscap-ing so distinctive that the grounds have been registered as an official U.S. Botanical Garden. The marvelous mix of sophistica-tion and relaxation makes this urban resort unique among Caribbean casino hotels. The architecture and especially the interior design play a major part in creating El San Juan's distinctive ambience.

Tucked into a corner of the lobby, the French Bistro offers sidewalk cafe-style seating and ambience, serving breakfast croissants and light foods and desserts into the evening.

Lavish, Old World style lends El San Juan's lobby bar, casino, and other public spaces an aura of sophistication.

[below] Located next to the casino entrance, the hotel's new cigar bar maintains the exquisite style found in the original parts of the hotel, while new computer-controlled humidifiers and a special ventilation system provide the best possible atmosphere for sampling the bar's hand-rolled specials. The bar back is lined with private cigar humidors.

A view of the free-form pool with swim-up bar illustrates that this very urbane resort also possesses a wonderful beach, and inspiring views of the sea and sky.

[below] These elegantly crafted stairs lead from the hotel lobby to the ballroom.

The Royal Suite once belonged to a single wealthy guest who used it regularly. Lalique chandeliers, marble columns, Chinese scatter rugs, and rich mahogany furniture lend the suite the ambience of a posh private apartment.

[left] Adjacent to the Royal Suite, the Celebrity Suite is dominated by a huge bed with an intricately hand-carved mahogany headboard and a chaise lounge finished with pale gray satin brocade.

RITZ-CARLTON SAN JUAN HOTEL AND CASINO

Architecture by Nichols Brosch Sandoval
Interior design by Hirsch Bedner Associates
Photography by Robert Miller

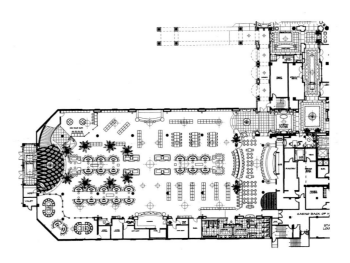

The casino displays elements of Old World Monte Carlo styling, with a dark elaborate ceiling treatment, elegant statuary and light fixtures, and columns topped with shiny gold palm capitals. The designer, Scott Perkins, describes it as a "Deco extravaganza."

The Ritz-Carlton San Juan is something of a hybrid property, for it serves as both business hotel and Caribbean resort. Located close to the airport rather than in San Juan proper, the 440-room property balances the sophisticated urbanity associated with the Ritz trademark with the less formal requirements of an outdoor-oriented resort while contending with the problems of the nearby airport. As architect John Nichols notes, "It's on the beach, but it's also near the airport and so the location is noisy. Thus the building turns inward, with fewer balconies than a typical resort. There are large courtyards and lots of meeting rooms, but it is not totally a resort."

Hirsch Bedner designer Scott Perkins puts it this way: "It's not an urban hotel, but it is primarily a business hotel, with a resort amenity." Given the beachfront location, in spite of the airport and the business slant, the hotel is "more casual than the standard Ritz," notes Perkins. The main difference, he says, is that the interior architecture features far less "English traditional" dark wood paneling; instead, the walls are finished with light-colored plaster, lending the hotel's public spaces and guest rooms a more casual, Italian- or Provence-influenced ambience.

With the casino on one side (with its own entrance) and the parking garage on the other, the symmetrical building is anchored by the centrally located reception lobby, which opens axially into a spacious main lobby that in turn lets onto a landscaped courtyard surrounding the swimming pool. As arriving guests move from the reception area into the lobby and the lobby lounge, glimpses of the pool, the landscaped grounds, and the sea beyond provide a sense of drama.

The Spanish colonial influence, toned down in the primary lobby areas, plays a larger role in the masculine designs of the

[left] View of the reception lobby and the lobby lounge show how the main public spaces are arranged on axis from entry to lounge to exterior courtyards and grounds, just visible through the floor-to-ceiling windows at the rear of the lobby lounge. The fixtures and furnishings demonstrate a fine balance between the formal style associated with the Ritz and the more casual requirements of a beachfront resort.

[right] Floor plan shows the Ritz-Carlton's symmetrical layout.

Light and airily spacious, this lounge area is set up for guests utilizing the gym seen through the doorway.

[right] The wood paneling in this boardroom lends the necessary air of *gravitas,* while the light walls and window treatments and the tropical upholstery send a more relaxed message.

cigar bar, with its exotic wood paneling—including Carpathian Elm Burl, Figured Fiddleback Etimoe, and Honduran mahogany—and carved Italian marble bar. The specialty restaurant, called the Vineyard Room, features a similarly rich design, intended to emulate the look of a "grand residence," according to Perkins. And yet, even here, the walls are pale plaster, because "a neutral palette tends to cool things off," says Perkins. An open kitchen lends an air of informality, with a black granite wall making a dramatic backdrop for the chefs at work. The boardrooms and other meetings rooms attain the same balance of Ritz formality and resort casual, with wood paneling providing the sophistication and cool plaster toning it down. Suites and guest

rooms share a casual, residential look, perhaps lighter and fresher than the typical Ritz to reflect the resort locale.

In the casino, Perkins says the designers were trying to "create a tropical Deco extravaganza, meant to evoke the grandeur of '20s and '30s Havana, or the look of a European casino." Large potted trees, metal palm tree capitals atop columns, a black and gold ceiling system, and non-glossy metal finishes all help create an effect that is "extravagant but subdued," notes Perkins—a description which might serve as the motto for the entire property: unmistakably a Ritz, but also unmistakably a beachfront resort. The necessarily delicate balance has been attained.

WORLDWIDE CASINOS *and* THEME RESORTS

Casino Designs Around the World

By Robert DiLeonardo, Ph.D.

In the game of life, nothing is certain. What might look like a sure bet one day can turn into a long shot the next. In this way, the art of designing casinos imitates life—it's a gamble. But, as any player knows, there are ways to increase the odds of success.

The sport of gaming has increased exponentially in popularity over the past several years, drawing an increasingly sophisticated and technologically savvy following. Appealing to the appetites of this growing audience has provided designers and developers with some unique challenges that have fired the creativity of both entities in ways never before imagined.

Casino design is no longer driven by the designer alone. Developers have become experts at concept. The casino designer with the winning edge understands his role as seer—as interpreter of dreams. He must embrace the developer's vision and use his expertise to translate that vision into a site-specific experience, appropriate to the location while fulfilling the customer's need for adventure and escape. The designer must understand the developer's concept and create, from virtually nothing, an artificial reality that transports the visitor to an exciting and stimulating fantasy world. The result must be a unified experience that at once reflects the concept of the developer while appealing to all of the senses of the end-user.

The designer's ultimate goal is to deliver the right product to the right market at the right time. This challenge differs vastly depending on the location of the casino. What works in Las Vegas will not work in Turkey or France. A Las Vegas development demands nothing less than a huge, dramatic experience; and many designers have become experts at recreating the ancient marvels and contemporary wonders of the world to satisfy the Las Vegas audience. However, in most non-U.S. locales, such mega-productions would be inappropriate and perhaps even offensive. A huge American experience would hardly be germane, for instance, in the Bahamas. Away from Vegas, design themes need to be culturally sensitive but not such a complete replication of the surrounding landscape that local users have no sense of escape from their everyday lives. Excitement must be delivered with a localized flavor with special care being taken to respect the customs and beliefs of the people who live there. The key lies in discovering some element of the culture that stimulates the senses and amplifying it to the highest possible degree, within the limits of taste.

Whether in Vegas or anywhere else in the world, the casino is experiencing a transformation into a complete entertainment experience. The casino's design, lighting, and accouterments are becoming part of that experience, stimulating those who enter its confines and enticing the visitor into the gaming rooms. The gaming element will, increasingly, become an amenity, with lounge acts, dining, spas, shopping, and other diversions contributing to the total entertainment package.

Balancing the fantastic with the pragmatic, of special concern to the designer are the specific business demands of the gaming industry. Security is of utmost importance. While intimate settings may be essential to the overall theme of a casino lobby, no area can be impregnable to surveillance. Gaming operations run around the clock, 365 days a year. Creating an operation that has no "down time" and where all public areas can be closely monitored has a dramatic effect on every aspect of the design from the planning of traffic patterns to the choice of materials. Yet, these issues can not impinge on the overall experience of being transported to another world.

In short, the art of creating a winning casino is as much a creative and technical balancing act as it is a game of chance. The completely successful design is on budget, on time, and serves the test of time. By keeping an eye on what's happening in the industry, continuously monitoring our end-users, and immersing ourselves in the culture of our locales, we can continue to delight and entertain existing and new audiences and stay ahead of the game.

Robert DiLeonardo, Ph.D., is founder and president of DiLeonardo International, an award-winning design and architecture firm based in Warwick, Rhode Island, USA. The firm has designed hotels, restaurants, resorts, casinos, and other hospitality venues all over the world. The firm's projects have been published in myriad design publications. An active leader and expert speaker in the hospitality industry, DiLeonardo has taught at Brown University, Rhode Island School of Design, and the Hotel School at Johnson and Wales University.

[left] Star City (Sydney, Australia) took an alternative approach in creating its sports betting area: instead of individual seating, it features an open design, perfect for socializing.

GRAND HYATT BALI

Architecture by Wimberly Allison Tong & Goo
Interior design by Hirsch Bedner Associates
Photography by Donna Day

Meeting the needs of modern international travelers while staying true to indigenous architectural styles is one of the great challenges for resort architects working in the exotic yet increasingly tourist-friendly islands of Asia and the South Pacific. On one hand, travelers want their air-conditioning, their satellite television, and their hot showers. On the other hand, when in Bali they want a realistic Balinese experience. The Hawaii-based firm of Wimberly Allison Tong & Goo (WAT&G) has decades of experience crafting resort hotels that rise to this cross-cultural challenge. With 750 rooms, multiple restaurants, swimming pools, meeting rooms, and recreational facilities, the Grand Hyatt Bali qualifies as a large-scale Western hotel with

all the amenities; and yet, by utilizing Balinese architectural styles and pan-Asian decorative motifs, the architects from WAT&G and the interior designers from Hirsch Bedner Associates create a property with roots in the region. In a sense, visitors here can have it both ways, lounging in contemporary, air-conditioned rooms surrounded by Balinese furniture that has been constructed to accommodate larger Western bodies. Though this kind of cultural theming and blending has its detractors, the Grand Hyatt Bali provides Western travelers with a colorful introduction to the religiously inspired arts and culture of Bali. If they want more, they simply head "off-campus" and find it.

The hotel draws on the idea of the Balinese village for its initial inspiration. Organizing the guestrooms into decentralized clusters surrounding informal courtyards, the architects evoke the local architectural style and create an enhanced sense of intimacy for the guests. Linked by bridges and interwoven with gardens, pools, waterfalls, and passages, the buildings feel almost randomly placed, as if they'd been

The stone-floored, open-air lobby overlooks the entire property with a dramatic view of the distant sea and sky. High, open ceilings allow heat to rise, providing natural temperature control.

[left] The porte cochère is linked to the open-air lobby by a bridge that crosses a lily pond. The structure was designed after a temple in the Balinese mountain town of Ubud.

[right] Site plan shows how the architects dispersed four clusters of guest rooms around the property to mitigate density. Each forms a kind of "village," with pools and garden pathways linking them.

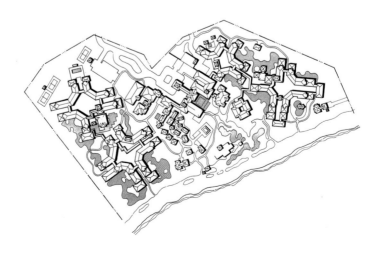

built over time, organically. To counter the sense of crowding in these "villages," the buildings are spaced to allow more air circulation between them; and rather than use the traditional Balinese thatched roof—impractical on a large-scale permanent structure—the architects specified red clay tiles, also in common use throughout Indonesia.

For the public buildings, the architects turned to other indigenous structures for inspiration. The porte cochère and open-air entry—and the lobby as well—draw on Balinese water palaces and temples for their forms. More specifically, the idea of crossing a pond to enter the lobby came from a ruined temple in the Balinese hill town of Ubud. Sited atop a hill above terraced ponds recalling Bali's thousands of terraced rice fields, the entry provides a dramatic viewpoint overlooking the hotel's guestroom and restaurant buildings as well as the beach and sea visible beyond the property.

To encourage guests to wander the resort's forty acres (sixteen hectares) of gardens, pools, and facilities, the designers distributed five restaurants—serving Chinese, Japanese, Italian, Balinese, and Malaysian cuisines—throughout the property. Each restaurant draws on the country of its cuisine for design influences. In lieu of a shopping mall, the design team created an area called Pasar Senggol modeled after Bali's lively, open-air markets, where Asian-style "fast food" as well as Balinese arts and crafts are sold. In the midst of Pasar Senggol, a local Hindu priest makes offerings and presides over ceremonies at a small Hindu temple.

Water is an integral element in Balinese culture, and the hotel's design reflects its importance—while providing guests with an enticing array of swimming pools, including the River Pool and Main Pool at the beach, the Balinese Feature Pool (designed like a traditional Balinese bathing pool), and myriad lagoons, waterfalls, fountains, and other water features.

Guestrooms throughout the property have been fitted with Westernized Balinese furnishings as well as regional arts and crafts for decorations, while the familiar comforts of satellite television and air conditioning put Westerners at ease in the Eastern-style accommodations. In the guestrooms, the designers have accomplished the same sensitive yet functional integration of East and West that distinguishes the entire property.

The open-air lobby bar's comfortable mix of Balinese- and Indonesian-style furniture customized to Western tastes illustrates the smooth integration of East and West that graces the property. The design team gathered decorative artifacts and statuary from all over Indonesia.

[below] View of the open lobby, surrounded by pools and gardens, designed after Balinese water palaces and temples.

Along with gardens and pathways, exotic water features include waterfalls, swimming pools, lagoons, and fountains, connecting the hotel's many buildings and creating a languid, appealing mood of tropical tranquility.

By gathering relatively low-rise, layered structures around courtyards and pools in informal patterns, the designers copied the look and feel of Balinese villages, establishing a more intimate scale for hotel guests. Red tile roofs are not Balinese but are used elsewhere in Indonesia.

[right] Portals and passageways often provide powerful ceremonial moments. The entrance to the Watercourt Cafe is flanked by elegant symmetrical statuary.

CHEJU SHILLA RESORT HOTEL

Architecture by Wimberly Allison Tong & Goo
Interior design by Ogawa-Ferre-Duthilleul
Photography courtesy Shilla Hotel Company

Collaborating with a Japanese designer based in Paris, France on this resort hotel on Cheju Island, Korea, the international architecture firm of Wimberly Allison Tong & Goo came up with a theme that qualifies as exotic—at least in Korea. The theme is Spanish Mediterranean architecture as it has been practiced primarily in California in recent decades.

View of the entry level main reception lobby illustrates the airy, California-style interior architecture, with Western furniture and Asian-influenced statuary.

Abandoning any semblance of Korean design at the request of the owners, the designers turned instead to Laguna Beach and Santa Barbara for their inspiration and made a building with Mission-style stucco walls, arched windows and doorways, and terra cotta tile roofs. Korean design might have had its appeal for an international clientele, but this hotel is specifically designed to draw a domestic crowd of vacationing Koreans, and for them, Santa Barbara style represents the height of contemporary, worldly sophistication.

With the furnishings provided by Junichi Ogawa, a sophisticated, Paris-based designer originally from Japan, the interior look is decidedly contemporary and Westernized, although the hotel offers Presidential Suites in both Western and Korean modes. This mix extends into the dining facilities, which include Korean, Japanese, and international restaurants, along with two bars and a bakery.

At the same time, the property meets the needs of Koreans. Three oversized banquet rooms provide plentiful space for traditionally enormous family gatherings, such as weddings, that frequently take place at the hotel. And the indoor/outdoor pool (Cheju Island temperatures range from quite warm to very cold) has little deck space around it, as Koreans are more modest than Westerners and rarely lie about in their bathing suits in public. And so, while the resort's designers succeed in providing Koreans with a taste of the West, California-style, they have done so without violating local customs, an important aspect of design in an increasingly internationalized resort and hotel marketplace.

[left] Cheju Shilla utilizes the Spanish Mediterranean-influenced architecture of southern California as the source of its themes and motifs. Two wings of guest rooms flank the central lobby and public space volume.

[right] California and Korea meet in this palm-lined resort that recalls Laguna Beach.

[above] The free-form pool begins indoors beneath the central lobby. The decks around the pool, both inside and outside, are smaller than they are in the West since by culture and tradition Koreans are much less likely to sunbathe in public and so need less deck space.

[right] The furniture and finishes in the suites reflect the taste of the European interior designers and the owners' request that the hotel serve as an exotic destination for Koreans rather than Westerners.

[left] Main level mezzanine overlooks the shopping area in the lower level lobby. The light, airy finishes and ambience were inspired by the Spanish-style architecture of southern California.

LE ROYAL MERIDIEN BAAN TALING NGAM

KOH SAMUI ISLAND, THAILAND

Architecture and interior design by RMJM
Landscape design by Belt Collins
Photography courtesy Le Royal Meridien Baan Taling Ngam

Positioned on a cliff overlooking the Ang Thong Marine National Park on Koh Samui Island's southwest side, the Baan Taling Ngam ("home on a beautiful cliff") integrates upscale Western luxury into a collection of rooms, suites, and villas that reflect the resort's remote island location as well as the indigenous architecture of Thailand. The primary public building—housing the lobby and other "public" spaces—

The open air restaurant balances rectilinear architectural elements with softening foliage and palms.

features a large, Thai-style timber roof and white-painted walls, constructed to step down the steep hillside towards the sea. Guest rooms adjoining these public spaces feature similar but smaller roof lines, while others cluster around the pool with its "infinity" edge designed to join it visually with the sea.

Every room in the main building is finished with a deck overlooking the Gulf of Thailand, the archipelago of islands, and the distant mainland. In addition to the forty-two rooms in the area of the main building, the hotel has seven beachfront villas

grouped around their own pool adjacent to the Mediterranean style waterfront restaurant. Another thirty-three villas are clustered in small "villages" around swimming pools, with coconut palms providing privacy screening. Every villa has a Thai-style timber roof and sliding doors opening onto wide balconies. The consistency of architecture lends the property considerable charm, while its upscale amenities provide high-flying guests with the necessary comforts. Like the best of today's indigenously inspired hotels, this one combines the best of both worlds.

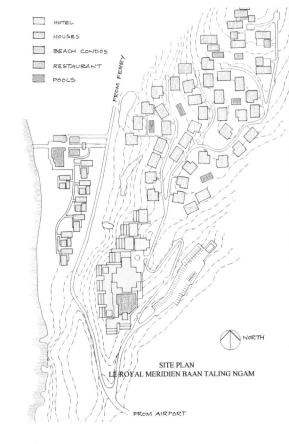

HOTEL
HOUSES
BEACH CONDOS
RESTAURANT
POOLS

FROM FERRY

NORTH

SITE PLAN
LE ROYAL MERIDIEN BAAN TALING NGAM

FROM AIRPORT

[left] The property's freestanding villas spill down the steep site to the sea. The architecture interprets traditional Indonesian design in a contemporary mode.

[right] Site plan

A temple-like form serves as a vertical counterpoint to the hotel swimming pool.

[right] The lobby area's appealing mix of tropical elements in an airy, contemporary design typifies the eclectic style of the resort.

East meets West in the hotel's spacious, beautifully appointed bungalows.

SUN CITY HOTEL AND CASINO

Interior design by Trish Wilson and Associates
Architecture by Burg Doherty Bryant
Photography by Strobe Photography

South Africa's gaming and vacation mecca, Sun City offers gamblers and tourists a medley of resorts, golf courses, casinos, and myriad entertainment venues, including the Sun City Hotel and Casino, designed by Louis Karol and built in 1979 in '70s modern style, with sleek, hard-edged Vegas interiors. More recently, after completing a makeover of the resort's guest rooms, the Dallas, Texas-based firm of Trisha Wilson and Associates brought its talents to bear on the hotel's and casino's public spaces, transforming the interiors into an appealing, African-themed "paradise island." Architectural changes consisted of minor reconfigurations of some public rooms; and yet the place has been completely reinvented.

The exterior of the building got little more than a paint job. Inside, the designers made up a story about leaving the South African bush behind to enter the paradise island of the hotel. The fantasy begins in the entry rotunda, where the designers installed a waterfall, man-made concrete rocks, and extensive artificial plantings to create an island jungle atmosphere. They reconfigured the reception desk and developed a sun motif in cast fiberglass panels for the wall behind reception. The sun logo also decorates the front of the custom-designed counter, and reappears in myriad locations throughout the project. A swinging bridge (with steel supports and beams) leads from the main lobby level to an upper level lounge, where dramatic lighting, lush plantings, and a canopy-topped bar combine to establish a playful tree house effect. To enliven the lobby slot machine area the designers added the Coin Fountain, a sculpture composed of 150 cascading fiberglass coins integrated into a waterfall and fountain set beneath a rainbow—as in "the pot of gold at the end of . . . "—representing the fortune to be

Colorful decorative birds and light fixtures, artificial plant-ings, man-made rocks, and waterfalls contribute to the festive jungle atmosphere surrounding the atrium slot machine areas.

[left] The casino entry entices players with walls, ceilings, and floors finished with stacks of brightly colored, oversized gambling chips, enormous brass coins, and other dazzling elements that hint at the fortunes to be won in the casino proper.

[right] The harlequin motif continues in the Harlequin Restaurant by the casino, where intense red tones, multiple interpretations of the harlequin diamond pattern, and another brightly colored mural help establish a lively atmosphere.

made playing the slots. A fiberglass ceiling made to look like the roof of a thatched hut extends the island theme into this area.

The fantasy of easy money explodes in color-saturated flash in the casino entry, where bright stacks of oversized fiberglass and resin casino chips flank the passage, more chips layer the ceiling, and the floor itself is finished with a multi-colored casino-themed custom carpet inset with enormous brass coins. Within the casino and the adjacent Harlequin Restaurant, another motif emerges: the harlequin (the joker in a pack of playing cards), celebrated most vividly in a hand-painted ceiling mural, and expressed as well via diamond patterns on walls and counter fronts. Complementing the harlequin, the sun motif established in the lobby re-appears dramatically in the casino, with gold leaf sun patterns on the doors, and gold sun medallions strategically placed on walls, soffits, and ceilings to hide security cameras and light fittings.

Other dining venues include the Orchid Restaurant, with an Asian interior suggested

by orchids painted on the walls and hand-carved mahogany millwork, and the African Grille. The Grille offers popular South African fare served in a space-themed in Colonial African style, with a painted ceiling vault framed within fiberglass panels cast to look like raffia matting (the wall finishes are real raffia), and cast fiberglass "bamboo" at the booths. Again, the designers did little interior architecture, instead depending on finishes and artifacts to establish the desired mood.

Adjacent to the Harlequin restaurant, a disco features state-of-the-art illumination, with prisms, multi-colored neon, and projection lighting, all computer-wired to the sound system to better match the music. A black granite dance floor and a black, high-gloss ceiling create a sleek, techno-pop space—a little island of hard-edged high style in the midst of the resort's generally more playful motifs.

The harlequin theme continues in a more toned-down fashion in the Salon Prive, the private gaming area. Mahogany paneling in a harlequin pattern lends elegance to the entry, while the floor evokes the sun with a

marble sunburst. Within the private salon itself, both the harlequin and sun motifs find their most refined expressions, with sun emblems in the ceiling used to screen HVAC and lighting equipment, and the mahogany and vinyl wall finishes provide a quiet harlequin backdrop for the artworks created specifically for the room.

Entertaining, playful, and even glamorous, the renovated Sun City Hotel and Casino has been given a new life with this imaginative makeover. Say what you will about the flash and fantasy of gaming design, when done well it creates an alternative reality wherein players can leave the real world behind.

The Salon Prive, a private gaming room for high rollers, interprets the resort's harlequin and sunburst themes in an elegant manner: the ceiling screens equipment behind fiberglass sunbursts in a grid pattern, while the walls are finished with mahogany wainscoting below and custom tufted wall vinyl with harlequin-patterned, mahogany crown molding.

The reception desk is made of honey-stained American maple wood with back-lit sun medallions.

[left] The "swinging bridge" leads to a tree house–themed bar on the upper level of the lobby rotunda. The bridge is actually made of firmly anchored steel supports, with pads, planks, and ropes added to the structure to give it some motion. The ropework, plantings, finishes, light fixtures, and bamboo all enhance the tree house motif.

[below] The entry to the Salon Prive includes a dazzling marble floor in a sunburst pattern that recalls the resort logo. The mahogany paneling continues the harlequin pattern, while the ceiling is a hand-painted mural of a sky with floating cards.

rows of blue Murano glass lighting fixtures. Above these rows of finely crafted pieces, windows etched with floral patterns rest atop panels finished with blue ceramic tiles and glittery, light-catching rhinestones. The etched windows serve as decor when seen from below; from the private gaming and slot machine areas above, they allow views of the main gaming hall below.

The upstairs slots and private gaming and dining areas reprise the essence of the decor below, with richer, darker tones and gold-finished ceiling panels establishing a more upscale ambience. Here and throughout, the designers have successfully integrated Islamic motifs and an informal, resort-influenced ambience into a lively twenty-four-hour-a-day casino.

Located just under two miles (three kilometers) from Istanbul's Ataturk International Airport, the modern high-rise Polat Renaissance Hotel offers travelers contemporary Western style rather than design deeply influenced by Byzantine or Islamic culture. Both business hotel and resort, the light, airy Polat contains 272 rooms with all the amenities business travelers expect: air conditioning, color television, direct-dial telephones, etc. The three-meal restaurant features an international rather than a local menu. Indoor and outdoor swimming pools, a health club, tennis and squash courts, and a shopping arcade enhance the international style of the project. The open quality of the design reflects the light-rich seaside locale rather than the culture of the region.

Those looking for Turkish or Islamic style in this hotel have to look carefully to detect these elements, which can be found primarily in the designs of furnishings, artworks, and finishes. Like many successful business or resort hotels around the world, the Polat Renaissance is designed in a contemporary, trans-national style that offers travelers the reassurance of the comfortably familiar, counterpointed with quiet hints of local culture.

[below] The double height main gaming floor features a palette of melon, amber, lavender, and pale blue. A back-lit glass ceiling with Islamic-influenced designs has the appearance of a skylight. In a gesture borrowed from Islamic style, the designers suspended rows of Murano glass light fixtures from a brass oval hung beneath the ceiling plane.

[below left] The designers specified Western-style interiors in a Middle Eastern locale.

Slot machine areas on the upper level feature the same cool palette as the main gaming floor. Curving coves and reflective gold foil finishes lend richness and depth to lower ceilings in the upstairs areas.

[left] Private gaming and dining are casually mixed on the upper level. The spaces feature an airy, western-style ambience, though hints of Byzantine influence can be glimpsed in the carpet design and other finish elements.

STAR CITY CASINO AND RESORT COMPLEX

Architecture and interior design by The Hillier Group in association with
Cox Richardson Architects and Partners
Photography by Patrick Bingham-Hall

Along with the Moroccan-themed high stakes gaming area, three high roller suites, or Inner Sanctums, feature three distinct designs: the Taj Mahal Room and the English Club Room, shown here, and the Oriental.

Star City in Sydney, Australia represents casino design of a type other than that found in the American gambling destinations of Las Vegas and Atlantic City. Given that Star City has a ten-year monopoly on gaming in Sydney, as Hillier Group architect and project principal Hank Abernathy points out, there is "no visual competition, and so we had no need to build the kind of stuff you see in Vegas or Atlantic City." And so instead of planning faux urban skylines, Egyptian temples, or other variations on the razzle-dazzle that lights up contemporary Vegas, the architects here responded to specific urban design problems unique to this multi-functional building and its site at one end of a rapidly developing mixed-use neighborhood.

The heart of Star City is the 156,000-square-foot (14,500-square-meter) casino and a 19,000-square-foot (1,800-square-meter) "high-roller" private gaming hall. Supporting the gambling operations, the complex also features seven restaurants, seven bars, two theaters, myriad retail outlets, a 650-seat meeting/function room, a 350-room hotel with an indoor-outdoor pool and a health club, lavishly planted rooftop gardens and plazas, and underground parking for 2,500 cars. All this—and an apartment building!—fits into a site between a low to medium-rise residential neighborhood and an inlet off Sydney's spectacular harbor, with a busy road slicing between the building and the waterfront.

Given the harborside location, it is fitting that the designers used water itself as a primary decorative element. Especially on the building exterior, water sculptures establish a dynamic, dramatic ambience. The Water Theatre, for example, includes three different water elements arrayed on three levels of the layered staircase on the harbor side of the building.

The casino is divided into four themed areas. The sports betting area features ceiling banners like racing silks and overscale images

[left] Sinuous curves and extensive glazing tend to soften the mass of the complex. Multiple decks and plazas provide exterior gathering places.

[right] Layers of plantings, sculptures, and structures form an array of appealing gathering places on the stairs that lead into the complex.

of athletic heroes. The other three motifs derive from the landscape: the Desert Outback; the Australian Sky (deep blue skies and night stars); and the underwater area, inspired by the Great Barrier Reef.

Since most of the traffic in the casino will be local repeat business, the designers built in a ceiling system that allows for frequent changes, particularly in lighting elements. And for the high rollers, a private gaming hall designed in a Moroccan motif can be reached via private elevator. The private gaming area includes three so-called Inner Sanctums, each finished in a different style: the English Club Room, the Taj Mahal Room, and the Oriental Room.

To further entice visitors Star City offers myriad dining experiences. On the same level as the casino, the Sports 2000 bar offers fast food in the midst of the sports betting action. Nearby, the Garden Buffet seats 475 in a stylized English garden setting. The Lifesavers Cafe overlooks the "underwater" section of the casino, with banquettes shaped like beach balls and rowboats evoking Australia's beaches. By re-creating the look of a well-known Shanghai restaurant, the designers made certain that the Palace of the Golden Moon would have an authentic look. Placed higher in the complex, three other restaurants offer upscale menus: Pyrmont's Restaurant offers grilled food in a space evoking a half-built ship in a shipyard, while the Italian-themed Porta Vista features retractable walls that transform the dining room into an open air terrace overlooking Sydney Harbor. And finally, the Astral Restaurant and Bar presides over all from its site atop the hotel, its elegantly finished interior of Thai silk, timber, and bronze offering intimate counterpoint to breathtaking views of the city, the harbor, and the distant Blue Mountain Range. A host of bars and shops provide alternative diversions, while the hotel and the two theaters help establish Star City as a complete entertainment universe, one with appeal to residents and tourists alike.

Located on the top level of a multi-story, outwardly-canted cylinder, a cool, glass-enclosed bar provides unobstructed views across the harbor. At night the cylinder glows like an enormous lantern.

Live coral reefs encased in custom made glass tubes add drama to the "Great Barrier Reef" section of the casino—especially when the divers enter them daily to feed the fish. The sculpted spiral columns, organic forms, portholes, and myriad glass bubbles overhead enhance the underwater effect.

[left] Gracefully contained within this curving gold wall, the lowest element in the Water Theatre features ninety individually controlled water jets that pulse to create waves up to fifteen feet (five meters) high.

[right] This perspective shows how water sculptures and skillful lighting transform a monolithic set of stairs into a multimedia entry experience.

REGENCY CASINO

Interior design by Hirsch Bedner Associates
Architecture by Wimberly Allison Tong & Goo
Casino planning by Bergman and Walls Ltd.
Photography by Jaime Ardiles-Arce

The Regency Casino in Thessaloniki in northern Greece represents a successful effort by an American architecture and design team to join under a single roof two casinos, one devoted to the more subdued European style of gambling, the other offering the theatrical, fantasy-oriented American gambling style developed in recent decades in Las Vegas and Atlantic City. The building, too, is something of a hybrid, for it employs traditional northern Grecian (Macedonian) forms and finishes— a low-rise profile, hand-troweled stucco walls, red tile roofs, and wooden shutters, doors, and windows—in a state-of-the-art, ultra-contemporary casino. According to WAT&G architect Michael Paneri, "the form suggests an irregular series of structures

built over time, while variety in building shapes and roof geometry creates an unusual mixture of building masses. Outdoor terraces, courtyards, and balconies offer guests a range of venues."

The interior opens dramatically with a domed rotunda entryway supported on pillars, with clerestory windows flooding the space with natural light. Gold tiles and mosaics add richness, with a central fountain reflecting the central dome and polished marble flooring weaving an intricate pattern around the fountain. After checking in at marble-detailed reception counters, visitors reach the casino by way of a passageway flanked by rows of classically proportioned statuary—an evocative, dramatically lit arcade of fragmented half-horses set on pedestals.

The 10,000-square-foot (930-square-meter) main gaming floor offers well-organized rows of gaudy, colorfully lit electronic slots and gaming tables, counterpointed by a lively design that makes reference to local building styles and regional motifs with wall finishes meant to suggest differing buildings, locally inspired decorative

Flanked by elegant, evocative rows of dramatically fragmented horse statues and illumined in part by light reflecting off an exquisitely finished gold ceiling cove, this passage leads from the entry rotunda to the main gaming floor.

[left] Drawing on local motifs, the designers created this domed entry rotunda, with clerestory windows permitting daylight to flood the interior, finished in gold tiles, and a lively, intricately patterned floor.

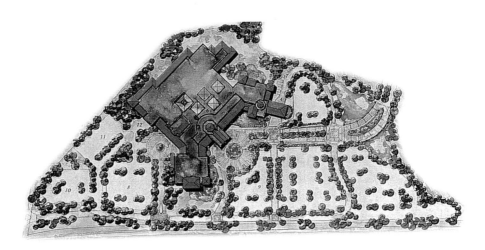

North Elevation
Guestrooms

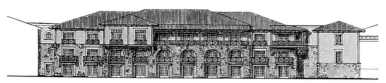

North Elevation

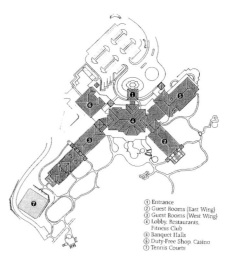

① Entrance
② Guest Rooms (East Wing)
③ Guest Rooms (West Wing)
④ Lobby, Restaurants, Fitness Club
⑤ Banquet Halls
⑥ Duty-Free Shop, Casino
⑦ Tennis Courts

patterning, and a sophisticated illumination program that highlights columns, wall decorations, and other elements as a means of visually scaling down the otherwise formulaic gaming floor layout. The carpet mimics local mosaic stone styles. The overscaled room also contains a centrally placed faux stone kiosk featuring a decorative tile bar on one side and arched windows on the other; again, along with its functional component, this structure serves to break up the expanse of the gaming floor. Of course there's plentiful flash and glamour as well, with signage and structures providing Las Vegas-style counterpoint to the regionally inspired elements.

The private, European-style casino is accessed from its own smaller-scaled domed rotunda, with an elegantly finished private salon providing high rollers with a quiet place to gather between gaming bouts. A marble-floored arcade borders the private gaming area, and an intimate lounge provides

a transitional space between the gaming floor and the specialty restaurant's dining room.

A larger cafe adjacent to the main casino is designed to evoke a traditional Greek outdoor cafe, with interior walls finished to look like the stone facades of streetside buildings. Back-lit windows and strings of lights enhance the garden-like effect. Open kitchens and casual furniture further the casual cafe ambience, as do rollicking Greek background music and a ceiling painted like a blue sky with white clouds.

With a dark, sleekly elegant showroom seating six hundred people for live performances—and plans for a hotel/conference center in the works—the designers have successfully mixed the flashiness of Vegas-style gaming and casino planning with a more subtle, upscale European approach, utilizing regional architectural motifs to integrate the diverse spaces—and to infuse the project with an appealing sense of place.

[above left] Color drawing shows the casino building in the landscape, with regionally characteristic red tile roofing and water features.

[above] Site layout shows how the casino relates to the nearby hotel and other elements of the resort.

[below] The main casino floor offers an interesting counterpoint of flashy fantasy elements and sophisticated lighting that highlights the decorative patterns and finishes, such as those on the columns and carpeting, which are drawn from regional motifs.

[right] With its open kitchens establishing the casual atmosphere, the restaurant by the main casino is meant to evoke a traditional Greek sidewalk cafe.

GRAND CASINO RIVIERA

Interior design by The Paul Steelman Companies
Photography by Ian Vaughan

Sharply detailed circus-themed murals of acrobats and clowns overlook gaming tables.

In the minds of many, European gambling begins and ends in Monte Carlo, with its ornate, Old World casinos, celebrity royals, and continental sophisticates. However, in other parts of Europe, for centuries gambling has been legal, and many hotels contain small casinos where patrons might play a few francs or pounds at a roulette wheel or a baccarat table. Beyond the James Bond buzz of Monte Carlo, the European gambling tradition is exemplified by these small subdued casinos, which have not, until recently, been designed with any sort of theme in mind.

In the last few years that low-keyed approach has shifted, and the flashier Las Vegas casino-as-destination design ethic has taken hold in Europe. Consider Cannes, for example. Famed for its international film festival, the French Riviera city has long been a resort of renown, with fashionable hotels lining its elegant shoreline drive. At least one Cannes hotel, the Noga Hilton, recently opted to install an American-style themed casino and hired an American firm, The Paul Steelman Companies of Las Vegas, to plan and build it.

Given Cannes' film festival fame, the design team from Steelman chose "the movies" as the thematic basis for the design of the Grand Casino Riviera. Located adjacent to the hotel's basement level convention and meeting facilities, the 15,000-square-foot (1,400-square-meter) casino features an array of themed entertainment and eating areas as well as gaming areas. Each space has its own distinct look, but they share an aesthetic that clearly owes its inspiration to the film industry. With the flash and glitter of movies, movie stars, and Hollywood hoopla driving the design, Steelman's team set out to create a "multiple entertainment experience" unlike anything

[left] The passageway to the registration vestibule features a line of oversized cast-fiberglass chorus girls leaning over to form an arch; their reflections in a mirrored wall, opposite, double the dramatic impact.

[right] An intricately detailed ceiling sets the movie-like theme of La Grand Adventure gaming room.

ence" unlike anything the Europeans had seen before—excepting those who'd been to Las Vegas, of course.

The casino vestibule opens into two directions: to the left lies an area called La Grande Revue, an Art Deco–styled slot machine salon done up to recall the Busby Berkeley musical of Hollywood's Golden Age, the 1930s. But first, casino patrons must register—all gamblers are required to register before entering a casino in France—and the hallway to registration, known as "La Grande Danse," consists of a spectacular visual event: a line of oversized cast fiberglass chorus girls leaning over to form an arch down one side of the aisle, reflected in mirrors to double the dramatic impact. At the end of this passage, the registration lobby has been styled to resemble a 1930s movie palace with floral carpeting and faux stone columns trimmed with gold and topped with gilded leaf capitals. Suspended from the center of the ceiling, a grandly scaled light fixture of metal leaves and multi-colored glass illuminates the room with gilded cinematic splendor.

Three gaming rooms occupy the main part of the casino. The largest is known as La Grande Adventure, consisting of an expansive table gaming space that has been decorated like the set of an Indiana Jones adventure movie, with faux stone columns crowned with flame capitals supporting a sky blue ceiling over a network of faux textured beams from which drape bougainvillea plants. The two-level space also features a forty-seat dining area and lounge, divided from the gaming area by a low rock wall. A wall mural of a mountain landscape visually expands the windowless internal space; in that it looks like a movie backdrop, it, too, enhances the cinematic theme. Also accessed from the registration vestibule is the Studio Festival entertainment lounge, a space designed as a tribute to Hollywood

musicals, with gold CD tabletops, video screens, dance platforms, and stages establishing the musical ambience. The most intimate gaming area is Le Grand Cirque, a gaming table salon that suggests the atmosphere inside a circus tent, complete with murals of acrobats and harlequin-patterned columns topped with elephant head capitals. By employing the multi-faceted idea of "the movies" as thematic source, the designers opened up a world of diverse motifs to play with; the colorful variety of experiences in this casino reflects this amusing diversity.

"La Grand Adventure," the casino's bi-level main gaming floor, has been designed to resemble a set for an imagined adventure movie in the Indiana Jones mode, with faux stone columns, flaming capitals, a sky blue ceiling set off by textured beams, and draped plantings creating an exotic ambience.

The intimate gambling salon, Le Grand Cirque, resembles the interior of a circus tent. The columns are finished in a harlequin pattern and crowned with elephant head capitals.

[left] Elephant head capitals enhance the circus theme in Le Grand Cirque.

CASINO DE DEAUVILLE

Interior design by Hirsch Bedner Associates
Photography by Jaime Ardiles-Arce

View of the entry lobby demonstrates how period-inspired furniture and lavishly detailed walls and ceilings evoke Old World elegance.

[left] France's Belle Epoque serves as the interior design theme, evoking glamorous times past.

[right] Constructed at the beginning of the twentieth century and recently subjected to a complete renovation and restoration, the Casino de Deauville displays a regal neo-classical bearing.

Founded by Napoleon's illegitimate half-brother, the Duc de Mornay, the resort at Deauville on France's Atlantic coast got its start with a racetrack built in 1862. The track drew the swells of Paris and London, and a few decades later, around the turn of the twentieth century, the Deauville gaming scene was expanded with a casino designed and built by Eugene Cornuche. The casino proved enormously popular, and has remained so for nearly a century.

After a hundred years of wear and tear, the splendid old building needed a major facelift. In spite of some trepidation that an American-owned design firm might transform the rather elegant casino with too much Vegas glitz, the current owners, Les Hotels Lucien Barriere, commissioned the London-based international branch of Hirsch Bedner Associates to undertake the restoration/renovation. Rather than go for the glitz, the designers engaged in a little historical research and elected to create a design based on the romantic imagery of France's Belle Epoque. And so the casino has been updated with the latest in gaming accoutrements, including a slot machine salon bathed in neon light, while the interiors overall have been burnished with a rosy elegant glow, evocative of glamorous times past.

Now, visitors enter first into the Grand Salon's entry foyer, graced with dual grand stairs sweeping up beneath an elegant crystal chandelier; rose-tinted marble and custom carpeting establish the refined

169

ambience. From here, smaller flanking salons provide access to boutiques, restaurants, and lounges, including the intimate restaurant, Les Cafe de la Boule, decorated with hand-painted murals and a stained glass ceiling. In the casino itself, a spectacular indoor gazebo, the Temple d'Amour, provides a focal point amidst the gaming tables. Throughout the project, the intimate rose palette, sophisticated lighting, beautifully executed details, and elegant finishes and furniture establish a refined atmosphere that harks back to more traditional gaming styles, while accommodating the flashier elements that spell success for contemporary casinos.

For European casino operators seeking to avoid or minimize American-style glitz, one of the real challenges comes in arranging the slot machine areas, which are by nature full of loud, tacky energy. Here, the designers created roof-like frameworks of light over the banks of slots, creating a dazzling, glittery effect but also organizing the machines into smaller groupings. High above, multi-colored neon lighting adds a glamorous glow.

[left] A rather imposingly scaled interior gazebo called the Temple d'Amour, or temple of love, provides a focal point—and beverage service—on the main casino floor. Lavishly detailed windows and wall moldings help establish a luxurious, refined atmosphere, steeped in intimations of elegance.

[right] From the new entry foyer of the Grand Salon, a pair of grand stairs contained within beautifully scrolled and detailed balusters sweeps elegantly upward; a crystal chandelier suspended overhead adds another note of Old World graciousness.

Casino Thun

Architecture and interior design by The Paul Steelman Companies
Photography by Ian Vaughan

The design inspiration for the Casino Thun comes from Monte Carlo and its glamorous historic resonance and rich thematic associations. The Las Vegas–based Paul Steelman Companies planned the lavish, classic-looking project, which includes the only sports theme bar in Europe, as a series of discreet spaces wrapped around a grand hall. Steelman's firm specified all the interiors, and then had the fixtures and other elements manufactured in the United States and shipped to Switzerland for installation. The firm also provided space planning and purchasing services, graphic design, and construction management.

Steelman interprets "Monte Carlo" here to suggest period-influenced embellishments, such as gold leaf, filigree, crystal chandeliers, an appealing trompe l'oeil ceiling mural, and other elements that establish a kind of sumptuous environment. Stylized murals of tropical plantings enhance the plush interiors with suggestions of verdant gardens, a tropical Mediterranean fantasy to enhance the Monte Carlo look. The elegant, relatively subdued decor is appropriate for the European market, which generally supports a more sophisticated type of gambling than that popular in Las Vegas.

[left and above] Rows of slot machines occupy the Grand Hall, the Casino Thun's central volume. Inspired by Monte Carlo and its classic casinos, the Casino Thun's murals and trompe l'oeil finishes add an element of colorful fantasy. Elaborate moldings, filigree and gold leaf detailing, crystal, and lavish carpeting create an atmosphere of sophisticated Old World elegance.

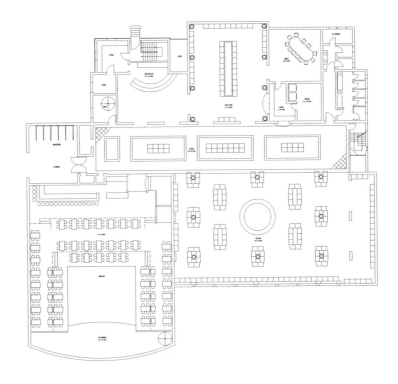

[right] First floor plan

CASINO LOCARNO

Architecture and interior design by The Paul Steelman Companies
Photography by Ian Vaughan

[left and above] Like Casino Thun, Casino Locarno combines a kind of upscale glitz with evocations of a tropical resort. Here, the flash and glamor is inspired by the Golden Nugget in Las Vegas, while the resort feeling is generated by the extensive use of silk plantings.

Constructed into the shell of an old theater, the Casino Locarno represents another fast-track transnational effort from The Paul Steelman Companies. After obtaining the commission from the owner/client and working from little more than a set of rough floor plans, the Steelman design team planned space, designed, and constructed the project in the United States; then shipped the components to Switzerland for installation. Remarkably, given the extensive amount of glass, the rather elaborate finishes, and the many curvaceous forms, the entire interior was built, shipped, and installed in just three months—and not a single piece of glass nor a mirror was broken in shipping.

According to designer Steve Anderson, the project's cream, white, and gold finishes were inspired by the original Golden Nugget in Las Vegas, a bastion of what Anderson calls "contemporary elegance." The bullnose moldings, soft curves, and sculpted fiberglass columns establish the elegant ambience; an undercurrent tropical mood comes with the extensive use of silk plantings. Beneath the serpentine ceiling vault and its profusion of foliage, ambient light sources establish a warm glow counterpointed by the sparkling dynamic of Tivoli lighting and myriad reflections off mirrored walls and ceiling coffers, marble floors, and brass details. The main casino is anchored by a central planter, linked to the adjacent boule room (boule is a European table game) by a meandering path—a path that, in the tradition of casinos, leads not to the entry/exit but simply meanders the casino floor.

Owned and operated by the same company that runs Casino Thun, the Casino Locarno shares enough design motifs to help establish a brand-name image for the company, as well as enriching the gaming experience.

[right] The casino features a private room for boule, a European table game similar to roulette. The mural evokes the mood of summertime in a tropical place, a lovely fantasy for midwinter in the Swiss Alps.

KAHALA MANDARIN ORIENTAL

HONOLULU, HAWAII

Architecture by Killingsworth, Stricker, Lindgren, Wilson and Associates
Interior design by Hirsch Bedner Associates
Photography copyright 1997, Kyle Rothenberg

When the Kahala Hilton first opened in the 1960s, it represented an attempt by Conrad Hilton to re-create the exclusive, luxurious ambience of the famous Royal Hawaiian on Waikiki Beach, away from the burgeoning development that had even then overtaken Waikiki. Located on the beach in the upscale residential suburb of Waialae-Kahala, the hotel soon achieved its sought-after exclusive status thanks to a successful marketing campaign aimed at celebrities and Hollywood stars. By the 1970s, the Kahala was nicknamed the "Kahollywood Hilton," and it had become the Hawaiian destination of choice for celebrities ranging from Frank Sinatra to the Rolling Stones. Naturally, the hotel suffered a little wear and tear over the decades, and so when the Mandarin Oriental took over the property recently, they felt an update was needed. And yet they did not want to change the hotel's well-established image or ambience.

To achieve this subtle transformation, Mandarin Oriental management hired Hirsch Bedner Associates. The firm responded with a design that changes everything and nothing at the same time. Public spaces and guest rooms in and around the ten-story 371-room hotel and its elegant free-form pool and inviting beach have been completely renovated without altering the essential resort luxe character of the property. The guest rooms integrate contemporary design with a theme that might be described as Old Hawaiiana with Asian accents, mixing teak and mahogany, handwoven Tibetan rugs, grass cloth walls, and local artworks. Bathrooms evoke a bygone era with vintage fixtures like freestanding mahogany vanity sinks with porcelain

The Plumeria Beach Cafe provides an elegant buffet for casual dining, serving three meals at a beachfront location. Slate floors signal a measure of informality. Dining tables spill from the restaurant out onto a patio close to the beach.

[left] The elegant yet informal lobby has been completely renovated and refurbished, but the sand-blasted sea glass chandelier still hangs as it has since the hotel opened in 1964. The sand and sea palette of the renovation also matches the original, making the changes less obvious.

[right] The hotel's signature restaurant, Hoku's, has been newly renovated with multiple levels that permit ocean view from every table.

faucet handles and hand-held bathtub showers.

Perhaps the most popular room at the Kahala is the lobby, an airy, inviting space dominated by a chandelier made of sand-blasted beach glass that dates back to the facility's 1964 opening. The chandelier remains, but the room has been completely refurbished—in the same sand and sea colors of the original, easing the transition from old to new. In addition to creating new and remodeled meeting rooms, the design team also totally made over the hotel's two dining rooms. The specialty high-end restaurant, Hoku's, has been designed with a multi-level layout providing every table with panoramic ocean views; the old Plumeria, its original space taken for meeting rooms, has taken up informal residence at the beach, where three meals are served in a casual, open-air setting. A new fitness center, a high-tech business center, and an arcade of shops complete the transformation of the 1960s jewel into a 1990s gem. And a new wave of celebrities now gathers around the hotel's swimming pool and on the beach. The Kahala represents that rare type of renovation where success is measured by how much has been changed for the better while seemingly nothing has changed at all.

Elaborate chandeliers and soothing wall finishes establish a festive tropical mood in the hotel's newly renovated meeting and banquet rooms.

[left] The grounds have been carefully landscaped to assure privacy for the famous guests. Water features include a swimming pool and a free-form lagoon that has been home to a pair of playful dolphins for over thirty years.

[right] The 371 rooms and suites come with views of the sea or the mountains. Rooms and suites have been completely refurbished in a style that combines contemporary design with elements of old Hawaii and Asia. The artworks are by contemporary Hawaiian artists. The palette is contemporary, balanced with rich fabrics and plantation/colonial elements such as the wooden shutters, teak parquet floors, and mahogany furniture.

SHERATON LIMA TOWERS CASINO

Architecture and interior design by The Paul Steelman Companies
Photography by Ian Vaughan

Colors and forms at the buffet evoke a nineteenth-century conservatory, with detailed murals of windows opening onto trees, gardens, and flowers elaborating on the fantasy.

Located in the Latin American metropolis of Lima, Peru, the Sheraton Lima Towers is a modern hotel with a design that owes its inspiration to the new internationalism in architecture rather than to any regional or locally driven design motifs. And so when The Paul Steelman Companies obtained the permission to renovate the hotel's restaurant and add a new casino, they soon discovered that the operators had no interest in evoking Mayan, Incan, or other regionally inspired cultural or historic themes. Instead, they wanted something sophisticated, aglow with Old World elegance. The Steelman design team looked to Europe for their motifs, and created a casino that would be at home in Monte Carlo—or even in Las Vegas.

Combining Vegas razzle-dazzle with upscale sophistication, the Sheraton Lima Towers Casino boasts of details like Austrian chandeliers, gold leaf trim, and elaborate moldings and other finishes evocative of nineteenth-century European gambling parlors. Though some might argue that such approaches betray the local tradition, one must remember that casinos and gaming are all about fantasy. The Old World sophistication and grace conjured by these generously proportioned, elegantly finished volumes are an exotic, appealing fantasy in Lima, Peru.

[left] The transition from hotel to casino is marked with a star inlaid into the floor and a circular ceiling dome overhead. Glittery finishes, elaborate moldings, and crystal chandeliers establish the rich Old World fantasy.

[right] Floor plan shows how the hotel lobby gives way to the casino entry.

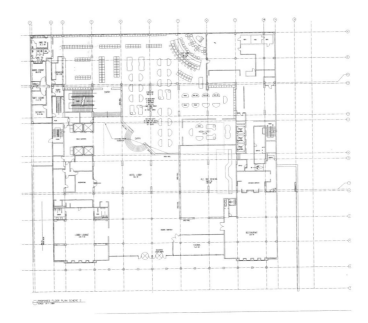

The main passage through the casino sets an elegant tone, seen in overview [left] and in a ceiling detail [above], beneath an arcade of luminous blue ceiling coffers enclosed by richly detailed moldings.

[below] Black, white, and gold finishes lend a sophisticated look to the bar, adjacent to the gaming floor. Note the literal Las Vegas glitz of the sign over the slot machines.

[right] Warm dark colors and textures, rich still-life paintings, and gold details including a gilded coffered ceiling create a voluptuous ambience in the semi-private high-limits gaming area.

MACTAN SHANGRI-LA RESORT

Architecture and interior design by Kanko Kikaku Sekkeisha (KKS) Architects
Landscape design by Belt Collins
Photography courtesy KKS Architects

An elegant 349-room resort combining Western-style upscale hotel architecture with indigenous design motifs, the Mactan Shangri-La's main building sits amid thirty-two acres (thirteen hectares) of landscaped gardens graced by a free-form, lagoon-shaped swimming pool. Counterpointing the medium-rise bulk of the hotel building, the food, beverage, and other facilities have been installed in grass-roofed huts finished in materials and colors that recall the indigenous architecture of Cebu, one of the most historically significant Philippine Islands. Beyond the landscaped gardens and pool, the property features a lovely stretch of white sand beach fronting aquamarine seas with coral reefs. Contained between a pair of jetties, this beach is perhaps the most striking element in this facility because it is completely man-made.

The guest room and lobby buildings rise to six stories, with sloping red roofs suggesting a residential mode. By stepping the buildings back, the architects lessen the impact of the mass and enhance the views of the Visayang Sea and outlying islands. For the interiors, the designers selected furnishings and finishes that meet Western expectations of scale and comfort while employing regional motifs and materials, including indigenous elements like bamboo and wrought iron, with its suggestions of the Spanish colonial period of Philippine history.

Surrounded by colorful landscaping, the hotel's free-form swimming pool recalls a natural lagoon and offers a curvaceous counterpoint to the rectilinearity of the hotel's guest room wings.

[left] Extensive plantings and setbacks help soften and scale down the bulk of the guestroom wings. Red roofs lend a hint of residential architecture.

[right] The lobby exhibits a successful blend of airily inviting, contemporary Western style with indigenous materials such as bamboo and cane. The wrought iron, carved woods, and shutters, on the other hand, recall the island's Spanish colonial heritage.

CREDITS

Las Vegas and Lake Tahoe, Nevada

The Mirage and Treasure Island Resorts
Las Vegas, Nevada

Architecture, interior design, and conceptual design by Mirage Resorts
Photography copyright Mirage Resorts, Inc.

New York-New York Hotel and Casino
Las Vegas, Nevada

Architecture by Gaskin and Bezanski
Interior design by Yates, Silverman; project designer: Joyce Orias, AIA
Photography copyright New York-New York Hotel and Casino

Sunset Station Hotel and Casino
Las Vegas, Nevada

Architecture and interior design by Morris and Brown, William F. Morris, president.
Consultants: Tiberti Construction, general contractor; Martin and Peltyn Inc., structural engineer; Martin and Martin Inc., civil engineer; AE Associates Inc., mechanical engineer; MSA Engineering Inc., electrical engineer; Kimley-Horn, traffic engineer; J.W. Zunino and Associates, landscape architect; TMA Inc., communications consultant; F.S.A. Design, food and beverage systems design; Sign Systems, Inc., signage; Western Technologies Inc., geo tech
Photography by Marc Reynolds

The Desert Inn Resort and Casino
Las Vegas, Nevada

Interior design consultations and renovations by Hirsch Bedner Associates and The Paul Steelman Companies
Photography by Robert Miller

Caesar's Palace Tower
Las Vegas, Nevada

Architecture by Bergman Walls and Youngblood in association with Wimberly Allison Tong & Goo
Interior design by Wilson and Associates
Consultants: Pernini Building company, general contractor; James Adams Design, theming designer; Lifescapes International Inc., landscaping; Martin and Peltyn Inc., structural engineers; Martin and Martin, civil engineers
Photography by Peter Malinowski, InSite Architectural Photography

Harrah's High Limit Casino and Lounge
Lake Tahoe, Nevada

Architecture and interior design by Creative Resource Associates, Richard Licatta, AIA, production architect; CRA project team: Fernando de Moraes, Hydee Hirschmann, Hea Sook Kim, Julia Glass, Jihee Rowe, Jennifer Stewart
Consultants: Q&D Construction, general contractor; Dinter Engineering, engineer; Daniel Fine Art, art consultant
Photography by Robert Miller

Luxor Hotel and Casino
Las Vegas, Nevada

Architectural renovation by Klai:Juba Architects
Interior design renovation by Dougall Design Associates Inc. (public spaces, rooms, and standard suites)
Luxury suite renovation by Anita Brooks/Charles Gruwell Interior Design International
Consultants: Circus Circus Development, contractor and purchaser
Suite and exterior photographs copyright Circus Circus Enterprises Inc.; interiors copyright Dougall Design

Rio Suite Hotel and Casino
Las Vegas, Nevada

Architecture, interior design, and general contracting by Marnell Corrao Associates Ltd.
Photography copyright Rio Suite Hotel and Casino

Monte Carlo Hotel and Casino
Las Vegas, Nevada

Architectural concept and interior design by Dougall Design Associates Inc.
Photography copyright Circus Circus Enterprises Inc.

Riverboats and Terminal Pavilions

Showboat Mardi Gras Casino
East Chicago, Indiana

Architecture and interior design: The Hillier Group, Bittner and Detela (associate architect), Robert E. Curtin, AIA (design consultant for Showboat Operating Company) Showboat design team: Robert E. Curtin, AIA, design and architectural team leader; Tom Gourguechon, project control manager; The Hillier Group design team: Robert Blakeman, AIA, project principal; Karen Babb, interior design lead; Peter Hoppner, AIA, architectural design lead; Rom Rheaume, AIA, project architect and land-based project manager; Peter Morgan, AIA, project manager, vessel.

Consultants: Tonn and Blank, contractor; The Kern Organization, sculptural castings; Evergreen Studios, murals; Rodney E. Lay and Associates, naval architect; Atlanta Marine, vessel construction

Photography by Richard Lanega

Argosy Casino Terminal Building and Gaming Boat
Riverside, Missouri

Architecture: WRS Architects Inc. design team: Ron Reid, David Reid, Ralph Keys, Larry Alexander, Chuck Adams, David Haase-Divine, Aaron Zimmerman, Terry Berkbuegler

Interior design: Anderson/Miller Inc. design team: Pam Anderson, Laurie Miller, Jodi Caticchio, Dan Sedlock, Krista Boersma; gaming boat interior design: Interior Design International

Consultants: Yarnell Associates, lighting design; Kiku Obata and Company, graphics consultant; A.T. Renczarski and Co., structural engineer; Smith and Boucher consulting engineers, mechanical/electrical engineers

Photography copyright Mike Sinclair

Port Argosy Pavilion and Gaming Boat
Lawrenceburg, Kansas

Concept by Argosy Gaming Company

Lead designer: American Consulting Engineers; design team: Jim Wurster, Mike Marinaro, Jim Peck, Mike Hoopingarner, Chuck Schaeffler, Janet Sterling, Jim Breitinger, Dave Day, Max Newkirk, Steve Hanscom

Project artistic director: Lenzy Hendrix; associate architect: Ratio Architects; design team: Steve Risting, Dave Rausch, Dave Smith, Bob McGill, Mike Bivens; interior design: designplan Inc. design team: Lenzy Hendrix, Lori Hovarth, Jill Willey

Consultants: Ross and Baruzzini, mechanical, electrical, and plumbing engineering; Simmons J. Barry and Associates, marine/harbor engineering; Gulf Engineers and Consultants, associate marine engineer; Sherman Robinson Inc., food service design; RQAW, garage design; Jones and Phillips, Assoc., lighting design; Thunder and Lightning, lighting effects; Willey + Associates, interior graphics; Plancom, Inc., exterior wayfinding/graphics; Ralph Gerde Consultants, code consultant; Plum, Klausmeir, Gehrum, traffic engineering; Earth Source, wetland design; F.D.R. Engineering, city dock engineering; ATC Environmental, geotechnical engineering; Cultural Resource Analysts, archeological consultants; KZF, Inc., Spirit of America barge design; Zounds Productions, sound design; Muller, Traintafillou Associated Design, visual simulations; TGWB, three-dimensional renderings; Vaughn Crombie, concept renderings; Messer Acme, construction management.

Artistic Team: Setup and Co, castings; Ahrens Studio, stainglass overlay; Godward Glass, Todd Riefers, Nick Riefers, Indiana Art Glass, Butler Art Graphics, Walter Knabe Studio

Photography by Amy Henning Jobst (except where otherwise noted by Mike Krider, Krider Studio)

Harrah's Shreve Star Riverboat Casino
Shreveport, Louisiana

Architecture and interior design by The Paul Steelman Companies

Photography by Ian Vaughan

Native American Casinos

Mohegan Sun Casino
Uncasville, Connecticut

Architecture by Brennan Beer Gorman/Architects

Concept and interior design: Rockwell Group; design team: David Rockwell, principal; Jay Valgora, director of design; Paul Vega, David Fritzinger, Suzanne Couture, Masako Fukuoka, Linda Laucirica, Julia Roth, Eve-Lynn Schoenstein, Jeanne Valdez, Alice Yiu, interior design; Carl D'Alvia, Robert Ashton, Ehab Azmy, Alex Brown, Howard Chang, Rosa Maria Colina, Eric Epstein, Maria Teresa Genoni-Alvarez, Niels Guldanger, Chin Lee, David Lefkowitz, Alex Li, David Mexico, Tom Pedrazzi, Chris Pollard, Joe Richvalsky, Rober Robinowitz, Alex Ross, Sally Ross, Michelle Segre, Paul Shurtleff, Michael Silver, Nina Stern, Cathy Taylor, Raymond Tom, Sam Trimble, David Wilbourne, Lorrin Wong, staff; design team: Hank Brennan, AIA, partner-in-charge; Mario LaGuardia, AIA, Marc Gordon, Alan Infante, Nick Baratto, Greg Galford, Ernie Acosta, Sarge Gardiner, Louis DiFusco, Marlon Fernandez, Tony Layco, Ed Descalzo, Katie Brennan Smith.

Consultants: DeSimone, Chaplin and Dobrin, structural engineers; Lehr Associates, mechanical, electrical, plumbing engineers; Mohegan Tribe, tribal; EDSA, landscape; Focus Lighting, lighting; David Jacobson Associates, casino; Morse Diesel, construction

Photography by Paul Warchol

Harrah's Skagit Valley Casino
Skagit Valley, Washington

Architecture and interior design by The Paul Steelman Companies

Photography by Ian Vaughan

Harrah's Ak-Chin Casino
Phoenix, Arizona

Architecture and interior design by The Paul Steelman Companies

Photography by Ian Vaughan

CARIBBEAN RESORTS WITH CASINOS

 WESTIN RIO MAR
RESORT AND
COUNTRY CLUB
Rio Grande, Puerto Rico

Architecture: Sierra Cardona Ferrer project team: Luis Sierra Segundo Cardona, Alberto Ferrer, Edgardo Perez; architectural consultant: Alan Lapidus project team: Alan Lapidus, John Bowstead, Patricia Aidea

Interior design, graphics: Hirsch Bedner Associates Project team: Howard Pharr, Holly Kappes, Alan Russel, Alan Osborn, Marla Mayfield

Consultants: Tishman Construction Corporation, general contractor; Leonard Parker Company, purchasing; PHA/Paul Helms Associates, lighting; Roberto Pacifico Associates, kitchen consultant; CMA, engineering; Willowbend Land Design, landscape/site planning

Photography by Durston Saylor

 HYATT REGENCY ARUBA
Aruba, West Indies

Architecture: Thompson, Ventulett, Stainback and Associates

Interior design, graphics: Hirsch Bedner Ballast Nedam Groep, NV, contractor; PHA Lighting design, lighting; Edward Stone Jr. and Associates, landscape; Art Group International, art consultant

Photography by Jaime Ardiles-Arce

 ATLANTIS RESORT
AND CASINO
Paradise Island, Bahamas

Architecture and site planning: Wimberly Allison Tong & Goo

Interior design: Wilson and Associates

Consultants: EDSA, landscape design; Cloward and Associates, water features; Crow-Jones/Bufete Construction Co., construction management

Photography copyright Sun International

 EL SAN JUAN HOTEL
AND CASINO
San Juan, Puerto Rico

Interior design and space planning: Jorge Rossello and Associates

Photography of Casino and Royal Suite by Robert Cerri

Photography copyright El San Juan Hotel

 RITZ CARLTON HOTEL
AND CASINO
San Juan, Puerto Rico

Architecture: Nichols Brosch Sandoval, Huyke Colon and Asociados

Interior design: Hirsch Bedner Associates

Consultants: EDSA, landscape architect; PHA Lighting design, lighting; Resort Builders, S.E., contractor; Leonard Parker Company, purchasing

Photography by Robert Miller

INTERNATIONAL RESORTS AND CASINOS

 GRAND HYATT BALI
Bali, Indonesia

Architecture: Wimberly Allison Tong & Goo design team: Sidney C.L. Char, AIA, principal in charge; Stanley Takaki, AIA, project manager; Henry T.Y. Kwok, project designer; local architect: Naokazu Hanadoh & Kazubiko Kuroka Architect, International Design Department, Shimizu Corporation

Interior design: Hirsch Bedner Associates Hong Kong; design team: Alan Stephens, partner in charge/design director; Carl Ettensperger, project designer; Barbara Teasdale, project decorator; Shimuzu Corporation, general contractor

Consultants: Shimuzu Construction, engineers; Art Guild Int'l, art consultant; Tongg Clarke & Mechler, landscape; David Carter, signage/graphics; Lightsource/Jeff Miller, lighting; Creative Kitchen Planners/Martin Kuralti, food service design.

Photography by Donna Day

 CHEJU SHILLA RESORT
HOTEL
Shilla Island, Korea

Architecture: Wimberly Allison Tong & Goo design team: Gregory M.B. Tong, AIA, principal in charge/project manager; George S. Berean, AIA, design principal; Henry T.Y. Kwok, AIA, project designer; local architect: Sam Woo

Interior design: Ogawa-Ferre-Duthilleul; consultants: Belt Collins & Associates, landscape

Photography courtesy Shilla Hotel Company

 ROYAL MERIDIEN BAAN
TALING NGAM
Thailand

Architecture: RMJM

Landscape design: Belt Collins

Photography courtesy Le Royal Meridien Baan Taling Ngam

SUN CITY HOTEL AND CASINO
Sun City, South Africa

Interior design: Trish Wilson and Associates design
team: Randy Huggins, Paul Duesing, Corinne
Wilson, Shiree Innes, Paul Buckley, Nessa
Tobin, Trisha Wilson
Original building architect: Louis Karol
Architect of record: Burg Doherty Bryant
Photography by Strobe Photography

EMPERYAL CASINO AND POLAT RENAISSANCE HOTEL
Istanbul, Turkey

Architecture and interior design: DiLeonardo International design team: Robert DiLeonardo, Ken
Bavaro, Tom Limone, Bob Macaruso, Bob Buss
Photography by Yavna Onar

STAR CITY CASINO AND RESORT COMPLEX
Sydney, Australia

Architecture and interior design: Joint venture of
The Hillier Group/Cox Richardson Architects and
Partners. Design team: Hank Abernathy, John
Richardson, project directors; Philip Cox, project
designer; Jenny Watt, project architect; Peter
Longley, technical director; John Ilett, casino
project architect, Mack Rawley, Tim Folland, the-
ater project architects; Rick Taylor, hotel and
apartment project architect; Brenda Nyce Taylor,
hotel and apartment interior designer; Richard
Desgrand, external works project architect; Tim
Jeffery, Scott Gordon, Scott Harrel, John De
Luca, Tim Howarth, Heleon Morrow, Steve Boyd,
Deena Ridenour, Michael Grave, Steve Hubbard,
Daniel McCahon, Tamara White, Ken Lill, Paul
Glesta, Quentin Parker, Susan Hodges, Jule
Beckingsale, Peyton Riley, Bruce Lincoln, Paul
Hemmings, Paul Sproule, Mark Davey, David
Radford.

Consultants: Vision Design, lighting and theater;
Landmark Design Group, theming designers;
Waterforms, water sculptures; Connell Wagner
Associates, mechanical engineering; Barry
Weiss Partners, electrical engineering; Ove Arup
Partners, structural engineering; Bruce Arundel
and Associates, plumbing and fire protection;
Michael A. Demling Associates, casino architec-
ture; Tract Engineers, landscaping; Emery Vin-
cent Design, graphics; Cini Little, kitchen
Photography by Patrick Bingham-Hall

REGENCY CASINO
Thessaloniki, Greece

Architecture: Wimberly Allison Tong & Goo, Herak-
litou 16, and Pandelis Massouridis AA Dip
Interior design by Hirsch Bedner Associates
Casino planning architect: Bergman and Walls, Ltd.
Architects
Consultants: Hellenic Technodomiki S.A., general
contractor; Frank E. Basil, C&M Engineering,
engineers; Lifescapes, landscaping; Maurice
Brill, lighting design; Designed Productions,
Marcad Design, theatrical lighting; CDS Associ-
ates, kitchen; IGT-Europe B.V., gaming equip-
ment; Designed Productions, audio
Photography by Jaime Ardiles-Arce

GRAND CASINO RIVIERA
Cannes, France

Interior design: The Paul Steelman Companies
project team: Paul Steelman, Clay Markham,
Susan Moore
Photography by Ian Vaughan

CASINO DE DEAUVILLE
Deauville, France

Interior design: Hirsch Bedner Associates
Photography by Jaime Ardiles-Arce

CASINO LOCARNO
Locarno, Switzerland

Architecture and interior design: The Paul Steelman Companies
Photography by Ian Vaughan

CASINO THUN
Thun, Switzerland

Architecture and interior design: The Paul Steelman Companies
Photography by Ian Vaughan

KAHALA MANDARIN ORIENTAL
Honolulu, Hawaii

Architecture: Killingsworth, Stricker, Lindgren, Wil-
son & Associates Architects
Interior design by Hirsch Bedner Associates Los
Angeles
Consultants: Kiewit Pacific, general contractor;
Applied Technology Corporation, structural engi-
neers; WGFS Lighting Design Inc., lighting; Fer-
ris & Harnig Hawaii Inc., mechanical engineers
Photography by Kyle Rothenberg

SHERATON LIMA TOWERS CASINO
Lima, Peru

Architecture and interior design: The Paul Steelman Companies
Photography by Ian Vaughan

MACTAN SHANGRI-LA RESORT
Cebu, Phillippines Islands

Architecture and interior design: Kanko Kihaku
Sekkeisha (KKS) Architects; landscape design
by Belt Collins, Hawaii
Photography by Kenchiku Gaho

DIRECTORY OF PRINCIPAL ARCHITECTS, INTERIOR DESIGNERS, AND CASINO DEVELOPERS

Argosy Gaming Company
219 Piasa St.
Alton, IL 62002
618-474-7500

Belt Collins, Hawaii Ltd.
680 Ala Moana Blvd.
First Floor
Honolulu, HI 96813-5406

Bergman Walls & Youngblood Ltd.
Architects Planners
2965 South Jones Blvd.
Suite C
Las Vegas, NV 89102
702-940-0000
702-940-0001 (fax)

Brennan Beer Gorman/Architects
515 Madison Ave.
New York, NY 10022
212-888-7663
212-935-3868 (fax)

Cox Richardson/The Hillier Group
500 Alexander Park CN23,
Princeton, NJ 08543-0023
609-452-8888
609-452-8332 (fax)

Creative Resource Associates
4200 South Sepulveda Blvd.
Culver City, CA 90230
310-839-2192
310-839-2198 (fax)

DiLeonardo International
2350 Post Rd.
Suite 1
Warwick, RI 02886-2242
401-732-2900
401-732-5315 (fax)

Dougall Design Associates Inc.
35 North Arroyo Pkwy.
Suite 200
Pasadena, CA 91103
626-432-6464
626-432-6460 (fax)

Gaskin and Bezanski
2235-C Renaissance Dr.
Las Vegas, NV 89119
702-451-6728

Hirsch Bedner Associates
3216 Nebraska Ave.
Santa Monica, CA 90404-4214
310-829-9087
310-453-1182 (fax)
909 W. Peachtree St.
Atlanta, GA 30309
404-873-4379
404-873-3588 (fax)

Huyke Colon and Asociados
GPO Box 321
San Juan, PR 00936
787-753-7151

Interior Design International
701 Dexter Ave. North
Suite 307
Seattle, WA 98109
206-284-2220
206-281-4366 (fax)

Kanko Kihaku Sekkeisha (KKS) Architects
17 Mori Bldg.
1-26-5 Toranomon, Minato-ku
Tokyo 105-0001 Japan
81-3-3507-0376
81-3-3507-0386 (fax)

Killingsworth, Stricker, Lindgren, Wilson and Associates
3833 N. Long Beach Blvd.
Long Beach, CA 90807
562-427-7939

Klai:Juba Architects
4444 West Russell Rd.
Suite J
Las Vegas, NV 89118
702-221-2254

Marnell Corrao Associates Ltd.
4495 South Polaris Ave.
Las Vegas, NV 89103
702-739-9413

Mirage Resorts
3260 South Industrial
Las Vegas, NV 89109
702-650-7400
702-791-7111
702-650-7401 (fax)

Morris and Brown
105 East Reno Ave.
Las Vegas, NV 89119
702-795-0906
702-795-0646 (fax)

Nichols Brosch Sandoval
161 Almeria Ave.
Coral Gables, FL 33134
305-443-5206
305-446-2872 (fax)

RMJM
1408-10 Q. House Asoke
66 Sukhumvit 21 Rd.
Bangkok, Thailand 10110
662-264-2130
662-264-2136 (fax)

Rockwell Group
5 Union Square West
New York, NY 10003
212-463-0334
212-463-0335 (fax)

Jorge Rossello and Associates
Almendares #2
Condado, PR 00907
809-722-2401
809-725-2990 (fax)

Sierra Cardona Ferrer
Metro Office Park No. 13, 2nd St.
San Juan, PR 00920-1712
787-781-9090
787-781-9095 (fax)

The Paul Steelman Companies
3330 W. Desert Inn Rd.
Las Vegas, NV 89102
702-873-0221
702-367-3565 fax

Thompson, Ventulett, Stainback and Associates
2700 Promenade II
1230 Peachtree St. NE
Suite 2700
Atlanta, GA 30309
404-888-6600

Trish Wilson and Associates
59 12th Ave.
Parktown, South Africa
PO Box 411297
Craighall Park 2024
011-447-6343
011-447-5355 (fax)

Wimberly Allison Tong & Goo
700 Bishop St.
Ste. 1800
Honolulu, HI 96813
808-521-8888
808-521-3888 (fax)
2260 University Dr.
Newport Beach, CA 92660
714-574-8500
714-574-8550 (fax)

Wilson and Associates
3811 Turtle Creek Blvd.
Dallas, TX 75219
214-521-6753
214-521-0207 (fax)

WRS Architects Inc.
120 NW Parkway
Kansas City, MO 64150
816-587-9500
816-587-1685 (fax)

Yates, Silverman
4045 South Industrial
Las Vegas, NV 89103
702-791-5606